1st EDITION

Perspectives on Modern World History

The Dissolution of the Soviet Union

1st EDITION

Perspectives on Modern World History

The Dissolution of the Soviet Union

Myra Immell

Editor

GREENHAVEN PRESS
A part of Gale, Cengage Learning

 GALE
CENGAGE Learning

Detroit • New York • San Francisco • New Haven, Conn • Waterville, Maine • London

GALE
CENGAGE Learning™

Christine Nasso, *Publisher*
Elizabeth Des Chenes, *Managing Editor*

© 2010 Thomson Gale, a part of Gale, Cengage Learning.

Gale and Greenhaven Press are registered trademarks used herein under license.

For more information, contact:
Greenhaven Press
27500 Drake Rd.
Farmington Hills, MI 48331-3535
Or you can visit our Internet site at gale.cengage.com

For product information and technology assistance, contact us at
Gale Customer Support, 1-800-877-4253.

For permission to use material from this text or product, submit all requests online at
www.cengage.com/permissions.

Further permissions questions can be e-mailed to permissionrequest@cengage.com

Articles in Greenhaven Press anthologies are often edited for length to meet page requirements. In addition, original titles of these works are changed to clearly present the main thesis and to explicitly indicate the author's opinion. Every effort is made to ensure that Greenhaven Press accurately reflects the original intent of the authors. Every effort has been made to trace the owners of copyrighted material.

Cover image Igor Gavrilov/Time Life Pictures/Getty Images.

LIBRARY OF CONGRESS CATALOGING-IN-PUBLICATION DATA

The dissolution of the Soviet Union / Myra Immell, book editor.
　　p. cm. -- (Perspectives on modern world history)
　　Includes bibliographical references and index.
　　ISBN 978-0-7377-4794-2 (hardcover)
　1. Soviet Union--Politics and government--1985-1991--Juvenile literature. I. Immell, Myra.
　DK288.D58 2010
　947.085'4--dc22
　　　　　　　　　　　　　　　　　　　　　　　　　　　　　　　　　　　　　2009043369

Printed in the United States of America
2 3 4 5 6 7 14 13 12 11 10

CONTENTS

comes the Commonwealth of Independent States and recognizes and welcomes the emergence of a free, independent, and democratic Russia. Bush also recognizes the independence of Ukraine, Armenia, Kazakhstan, Belarus, and Kyrgyzstan and recognizes as independent states the remaining six former Soviet republics.

declaration of sovereignty demolished the Soviet Union. When the Soviet Union lost Russia, it lost both its legitimacy and its only power base.

CHAPTER 3   Personal Narratives

how things have changed for her and others in the former Soviet Union because of perestroika and glasnost. She explains why she hopes perestroika will be successful.

FOREWORD

"History cannot give us a program for the future, but it can give us a fuller understanding of ourselves, and of our common humanity, so that we can better face the future."
—Robert Penn Warren,
American poet and novelist

The history of each nation is punctuated by momentous events that represent turning points for that nation, with an impact felt far beyond its borders. These events—displaying the full range of human capabilities, from violence, greed, and ignorance to heroism, courage, and strength—are nearly always complicated and multifaceted. Any student of history faces the challenge of grasping the many strands that constitute such world-changing events as wars, social movements, and environmental disasters. But understanding these significant historic events can be enhanced by exposure to a variety of perspectives, whether of people involved intimately or of ones observing from a distance of miles or years. Understanding can also be increased by learning about the controversies surrounding such events and exploring hot-button issues from multiple angles. Finally, true understanding of important historic events involves knowledge of the events' human impact—of the ways such events affected people in their everyday lives—all over the world.

Perspectives on Modern World History examines global historic events from the twentieth-century onward by presenting analysis and observation from numerous vantage points. Each volume offers high school, early college level, and general interest readers a thematically arranged anthology of previously published materials that address a major historical event, with an emphasis on international coverage. Each volume opens with background information on the event, then presents the controversies surrounding that event, and concludes with first-person narratives from people who lived through the event or were affected by it. By providing primary sources from the time of the event, as well as relevant commentary surrounding the event, this series can be used to inform debate, help develop critical thinking skills, increase global awareness, and enhance an understanding of international perspectives on history.

Material in each volume is selected from a diverse range of sources, including journals, magazines, newspapers, nonfiction books, personal narratives, speeches, congressional testimony, government documents, pamphlets, organization newsletters, and position papers. Articles taken from these sources are carefully edited and introduced to provide context and background. Each volume of Perspectives on Modern World History includes an array of views on events of global significance. Much of the material comes from international sources and from U.S. sources that provide extensive international coverage.

Each volume in the Perspectives on Modern World History series also includes:

- A full-color **world map**, offering context and geographic perspective.
- An annotated **table of contents** that provides a brief summary of each essay in the volume.
- An **introduction** specific to the volume topic.
- For each viewpoint, a brief **introduction** that has notes about the author and source of the viewpoint, and that provides a summary of its main points.
- Full-color **charts**, **graphs**, **maps**, and other visual representations.

- Informational **sidebars** that explore the lives of key individuals, give background on historical events, or explain scientific or technical concepts.
- A **glossary** that defines key terms, as needed.
- A **chronology** of important dates preceding, during, and immediately following the event.
- A **bibliography** of additional books, periodicals, and Web sites for further research.
- A comprehensive **subject index** that offers access to people, places, and events cited in the text.

Perspectives on Modern World History is designed for a broad spectrum of readers who want to learn more about not only history but also current events, political science, government, international relations, and sociology—students doing research for class assignments or debates, teachers and faculty seeking to supplement course materials, and others wanting to improve their understanding of history. Each volume of Perspectives on Modern World History is designed to illuminate a complicated event, to spark debate, and to show the human perspective behind the world's most significant happenings of recent decades.

INTRODUCTION

The Union of Soviet Socialist Republics, commonly known as the Soviet Union, covered about one-sixth of the world's land surface, spanned the two continents of Europe and Asia, and took in eleven time zones. It was the largest country in the world—more than 8.6 million square miles in all. That is more than the size of Canada, China, and the United States combined. It was what some called a "country of countries," because it was made up of fifteen union republics, twenty autonomous (self-governing) republics, eight autonomous regions, and ten autonomous areas.

The Soviet Union also was one of the most ethnically diverse countries in the world. It was home to an assortment of people almost as great as the land itself, ranging from Russians, Armenians, Moldavians, and Latvians to Uzbeks, Kazakhs, and Yakuts. Collectively, the more than one hundred ethnic groups living within Soviet borders spoke more than eighty different languages and wrote in four or five different alphabets. Twenty-two of the Soviet nationalities had at least one million members. To show how much they valued the minority nationalities, the state set up territorial homelands for most of the largest ones.

Ethnic Russians, Soviet citizens who spoke Russian as their first language and followed Russian ways, accounted for just over half of the country's 290 million people. The rest of the people were non-Russians from diverse backgrounds who kept their own customs and languages. About forty million ethnic Russians lived in non-Russian ethnic areas. Where they lived notwithstanding, they dominated in every activity throughout every part of

Soviet territory. They were singled out by Soviet nationality policy as the foremost ethnic group. It was telling that from the time the Soviet Union came into being until it fell apart in 1991, one leader and one leader only—Joseph Stalin—was not of Russian descent. Stalin was a Georgian.

Vladimir Lenin, the architect and the first head of the Soviet state, believed nationalism would disappear under communism and a Soviet people would emerge. Lenin turned out to be wrong. During the 1980s, 1990, and 1991, ethnicity and nationalism were major issues confronting Soviet leader Mikhail Gorbachev. Authors Theodore H. and Angela Von Laue in their book *Faces of a Nation: The Rise and Fall of the Soviet Union, 1917–1991* describe Gorbachev as an "ideological optimist" who "treated the ethnic and national diversity in his country as an asset." They explain that in Gorbachev's view

> The non-Russians had enriched Soviet society and world culture. Admittedly, there existed the danger of narrow nationalism, but socialism could solve all problems through equality and cooperation. The Soviet record was unique in the history of civilization, showing the benefits of interaction and rapprochement. Even the smallest ethnic groups had the right to their own language, with Russian serving as the common medium. All of the Soviet peoples were proud, [Gorbachev] inaccurately asserted, that they belonged to one big international family, "part and parcel of a vast and great power which plays such an important role in mankind's progress."

Gorbachev, however, had not anticipated the effect glasnost would have on the different ethnic groups and nationalities in Soviet territory. Glasnost was Gorbachev's cultural and social policy that encouraged open discussion of political and social issues and freer distribution of news and information. Under glasnost nationalist sentiments rose and many nationalities that for years had buried any thoughts of greater self-rule or independence began to express their true feelings. And, in some Soviet republics, with the rise of nationalism came increased ethnic tensions.

In an article that appeared in the June 10, 1990, *Orlando Sentinel*, journalist Charles M. Madigan defined nationalism as "the term given to the quest for secure borders, self-determination, ethnic languages and culture." He went on in the same article to dispute Lenin's belief that nationalism would disappear:

> Almost since the revolution of 1917, the nationalities question in the Soviet Union has been a menacing truth lurking behind the myth that 15 republics and 100 nationalities were unified by Communist ideology. What united the Uzbeks, Tadzhiks, Azeris, Ukrainians, Georgians, Estonians, Latvians and dozens of other ethnic groups was not common interest but a political philosophy imposed by force.
>
> Now that philosophy is melting away. . . . And all the old dreams of freedom and the ancient animosities between religions and ethnic groups are taking its place.

The first major flare-up of ethnic violence took place in 1986 in Alma-Ata, the capital of the Soviet republic of Kazakhstan, when large crowds of people gathered to protest Mikhail Gorbachev replacing the first secretary of the Communist Party of Kazakhstan with an ethnic Russian. When the government sent in ten thousand Soviet troops to break up the crowds, the protesters rioted.

Kazakhstan may have been the first major incident but it was not the last. Before long, ethnic unrest turned into ethnic violence, nationalism, and cries for independence. A case in point is Nagorno-Karabakh, an enclave of mostly ethnic Christian Armenians landlocked inside predominantly Muslim Azerbaijan. In 1987 citizens of the autonomous subdivision, which lay close to the border of Armenia, petitioned the Central Committee to be made part of Armenia. The committee rejected the petition, setting off demonstrations in Nagorno-Karabakh and in the Armenian capital of Yerevan. When Mikhail Gorbachev promised to set up a commission to study the issue, the angry Azerbaijanis protested. Large-scale fighting broke out between Armenians and Azerbaijanis, both of whom claimed that the Soviet regime in Moscow was discriminating against them. The following year, the issue was still a sensitive one and more ethnic clashes broke out. Concerned ethnic Azeris fled from Nagorno-Karabakh and Armenia to Azerbaijan. Ethnic Armenians, fearful of what might happen to them if they stayed in Azerbaijan, fled to Armenia.

In 1990, the Armenian government declared that the Soviet demarcation of autonomous jurisdictions was not binding on Armenians in Nagorno-Karabakh. When Azeris reacted by rioting, the Soviet government imposed a state of emergency in the Azerbaijani capital and sent thousands of troops to end the riots. The following year Azerbaijan began attacks on the Armenian population of Nagorno-Karabakh region and the Shahoumian district. Soviet Army and Azerbaijani special police troops rounded up thousands of Armenians from villages in Nagorno-Karabakh and in neighboring districts of Azerbaijan and deported them to Armenia. When the Soviet Union broke up, Karabakh declared itself an independent republic. The unrest and uncertainty did not end, however, and as late as 2009 no nation had formally recognized Nagorno-Karabakh's independence.

More than 20 years ago Soviet historian Yuri Afanasyev stated in *Time* magazine that "An enormous fire of national strife burns in the U.S.S.R." Even though the USSR is no more, his words continue to have a ring of truth. When centralized Soviet rule broke up, problems emerged in almost every Soviet region and republic. Some of those problems still exist, and ethnic and cultural differences continue to divide the lands once bound together under the umbrella of the Soviet Union.

World Map

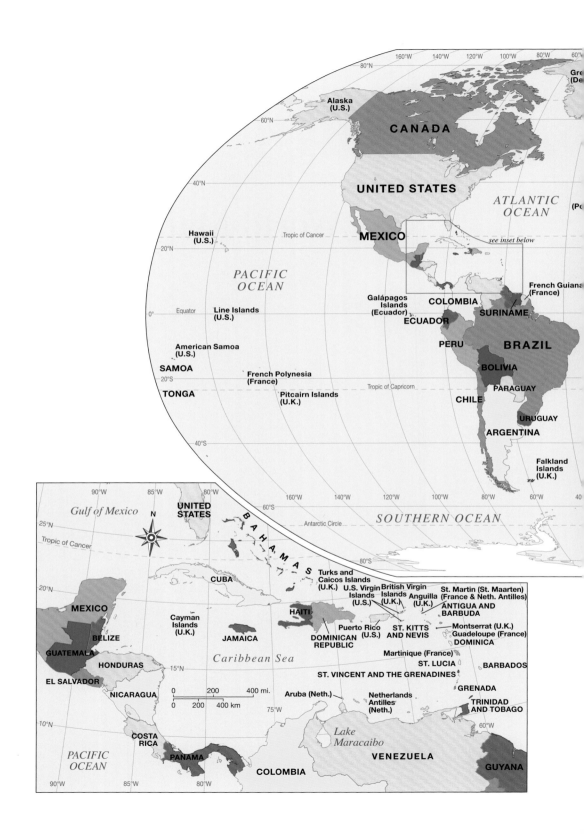

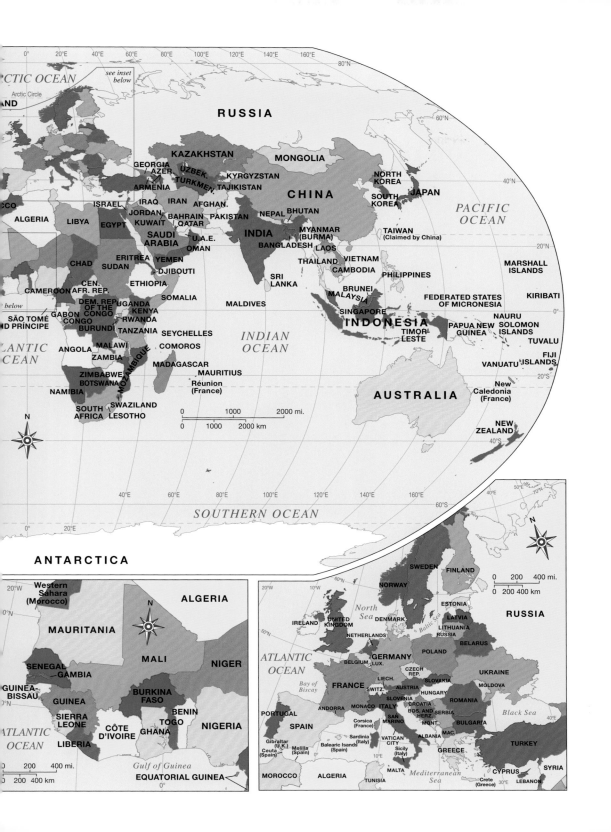

CHAPTER 1

Historical Background on the Dissolution of the Soviet Union

Rise and Fall of the Soviet Union: An Overview

Gale Encyclopedia of World History

The following viewpoint, excerpted from the "Union of Soviet Socialist Republics," *Gale Encyclopedia of World History: Governments*, introduces and provides a brief overview of the history and government of the Union of Soviet Socialist Republics (USSR), or Soviet Union. The evolution from czarist rule to the world's first Communist state took place over a relatively short but chaotic period between 1917, when the czar of Russia was forced to abdicate his rule, and 1922, when a treaty united the Russian Soviet Federative Socialist Republic with Ukraine, Belarus, and the Transcaucasus (Georgia, Armenia, and Azerbaijan). Over the next twenty years, the new entity, the Union of Soviet Socialist Republics grew to include other constituent republics in Central Asia and the Baltic nations of Latvia, Lithuania, and Estonia. In 1991, the reign of the once world

Photo on previous page: Vladimir Lenin expected Soviet identity to overcome nationalism, but vandalism of his image in Kiev by nationalists in 2009 suggested otherwise. **(Sergei Supinsky/ AFP/Getty Images.)**

SOURCE. *Gale Encyclopedia of World History: Governments.* Belmont, CA: Gale, Cengage Learning, 2008. Copyright © 2008 by Gale, Cengage Learning. Reproduced by permission of Gale, a part of Cengage Learning.

superpower came to an end, its Communist Party outlawed and its union collapsed and broken up.

The Union of Soviet Socialist Republics, or the Soviet Union, was the world's first Communist state, existing from 1922 to 1991. It was a one-party socialist regime, with the decisions of the ruling Communist Party carried out by a Supreme Soviet, a Presidium, a premier who served as head of state, and a Council of Ministers. The General Secretary of the Communist Party was the de facto ruler. The country's Communist era began with an immediate and radical program to establish a "dictatorship of the proletariat [working class]." This would serve as a transitional state between the formerly capitalist society—whereby the means of production are controlled by a few for their own enrichment . . .—to a classless society where all shared a nation's resources equally.

From the Czar to the Bolsheviks

Czarist Russia was ripe for revolution in the years preceding World War I. A wealthy class of nobles and landowners exploited those who tilled Russia's agricultural lands and had only been freed from serfdom some fifty years earlier. In the cities conditions were equally difficult for the urban poor, and the war caused even more drastic shortages of basic necessities like food and fuel. Revolutionary groups calling for social reform had arisen but were dealt with harshly under the czars. However, one party, the Russian Social-Democratic Labor Party (RSDLP), managed to survive as an underground group. In 1906 Vladimir Lenin was elected RSDLP president by a faction of his support-

> The new entity was named the Union of Soviet Socialist Republics (USSR), and over the next twenty years it would add—most often by force—several other constituent republics.

ers who agreed with his idea that a more radical approach was necessary to bring revolution to Russia. This split in the party created the Bolsheviks, . . . who favored Lenin's approach—and Mensheviks . . . , a group that argued for a more moderate path. A year later Lenin was forced to flee the country because of his political activities.

In February 1917 Czar Nicholas II was forced to abdicate by the Russian Duma, or parliament, whose members blamed him for the heavy losses the country was suffering on the battlefield and the near-famine situation at home. A provisional government was established . . . but it, too, struggled to maintain order among civilians and a disheartened, ill-equipped military. Lenin returned from exile in Switzerland in April 1917. . . . In October 1917, under Lenin's guidance, the Bolsheviks ousted the Provisional Government, and five months later Lenin—now elected Chair of the Council of People's Commissars—signed the Treaty of Brest-Litovsk, which ended Russian involvement in World War I.

New Government Structure

Civil war intensified in 1918, with anti-Bolshevik forces called the Whites fighting Bolshevik troops of the "Red Army" banner until 1921. . . . Finally, with the civil war quelled in 1921, Lenin and the Bolsheviks concluded a 1922 treaty of union that united the Russian Soviet Federative Socialist Republic with Ukraine, Belarus, and the Transcaucasus (Georgia, Armenia, and Azerbaijan). The new entity was named the Union of Soviet Socialist Republics (USSR), and over the next twenty years it would add—most often by force—several other constituent republics in Central Asia and the Baltic nations of Latvia, Lithuania, and Estonia.

There were three different constitutions that provided the framework for the Soviet state. The first one, in 1924, established the Congress of Soviets as the ruling body. Its members were representatives from local coun-

THE REPUBLICS OF THE SOVIET UNION

ARCTIC OCEAN

RUSSIA

ESTONIA
LATVIA
LITHUANIA

BELARUS

UKRAINE

MOLDOVA

KAZAKHSTAN

GEORGIA
ARMENIA AZERBAIJAN

UZBEKISTAN

KYRGYZSTAN

TURKMENISTAN TAJIKISTAN

Mediterranean Sea

Taken from: Arizona Geographic Alliance, Department of Geography, Arizona State University.

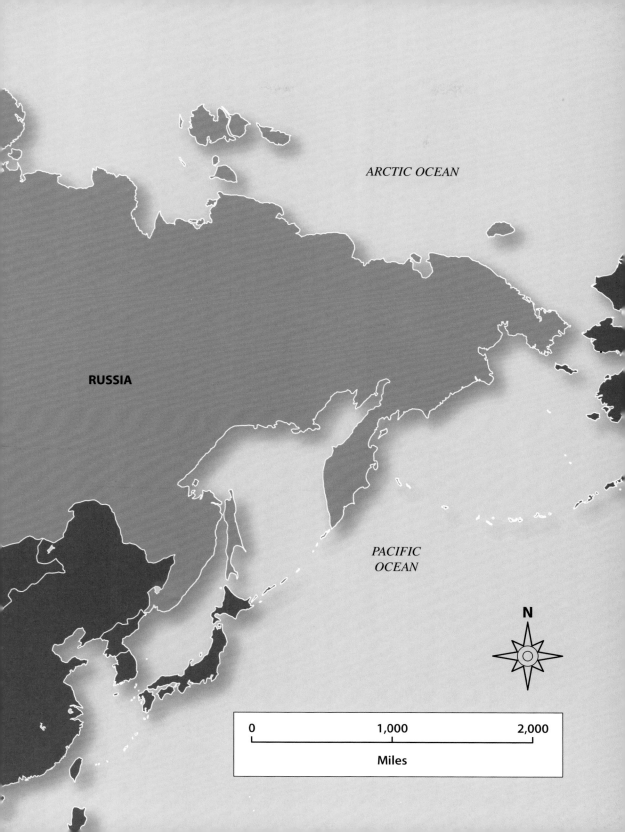

Some former citizens venerated the USSR—and its founders—long after its fall. (Gent Shkullaku/ AFP/Getty Images.)

cils (*soviets*), made up of workers and peasants but fully controlled by the Communist Party, as the Bolshevik organization renamed itself. . . .

The 1936 Constitution differed markedly from its predecessor. It eliminated the Congress of Soviets, guaranteed Soviet citizens the rights to work and to an education, and also ensured their medical care, housing needs, and old-age pensions. At the time, no other constitution in the world provided such economic assurances to its people. Ruling power was to be invested in the All-Russian Central Executive Committee, now renamed the Supreme Soviet. . . .

Each of the individual republics had their own Supreme Soviets. . . .

A new constitution went into effect in 1977. It asserted that the goals of the dictatorship of the pro-letariat had been met, that workers and peasants no longer needed their interests protected by the state from exploitation, and in effect the Soviet state was the Soviet people. As with the previous documents, civil liberties such as freedom of speech, of religion, and of assembly were protected—so long as they did not infringe upon the goals of the state or tenets of the Communist Party, which the 1977 Constitution described [as] the "leading and guiding force" of the state. . . .

> The death of Lenin in 1924 was the first milestone in the history of the fully formed Soviet state.

In 1989 a new legislature was created that resurrected the Congress of Soviets of the 1930s. The election of its membership marked the first tentative steps toward a multiparty system. . . . Only one legislative election was ever held in the Soviet Union, however, in March 1989, but it was the first time that new political parties had been allowed to form and participate in the electoral process.

Before reforms were enacted in 1989, Soviet political institutions merely carried out the policies and directives of the Communist Party. The party's executive leader-ship committee made all decisions, and government bodies "voted" their approval to provide a veneer of legitimacy. Renamed the Communist Party of the Soviet Union (CPSU) in 1952, the party ruled every aspect of Soviet life. . . .

Stalin and the Great Fatherland War

The death of Lenin in 1924 was the first milestone in the history of the fully formed Soviet state. A Georgian Communist named Joseph Stalin had risen within party ranks and was already serving as General Secretary of the Party at the time of Lenin's death, but that post did not yet carry the influence it later would. By ruthlessly eliminating threats to his leadership, Stalin came to control the state as well as the party by 1928. . . . His economic policies, including the forced collectivization of farmland, caused widespread famine in the western parts of the Soviet Union, but his leadership during World War II made him an ally of the United States and Great Britain in their fight against Nazi Germany. Known as the Great Fatherland War, the 1939–45 conflict was especially hard on the Soviet people, which lost nearly an eighth of its population, or twenty million people, from civilian and military casualties combined.

> The control of the CPSU [Communist Party of the Soviet Union] over a population of 293 million Soviet citizens across 8.6 million square miles was unprecedented in human history.

The Allied victory in 1945 gave the Soviet Union an opportunity to widen its sphere of influence. . . . By 1948 Poland, Czechoslovakia, Hungary, Romania, Bulgaria, and even the Soviet-occupied quartile of Germany declared themselves one-party socialist states. . . .

The Gorbachev Era

In 1985 Mikhail Gorbachev became General Secretary of the CPSU and de facto leader of the Soviet Union, following a long line of stolid, often elderly party hardliners who ruled after Stalin's death in 1953. The new Soviet leader stunned a world long dominated by Cold War politics between the Soviet Union and . . . the United States, by introducing a series of reforms that were publicized by two catchwords, *glasnost* (openness) and *perestroika* (restructuring). Glasnost was aimed at reducing . . . bureaucratic corruption, partly by allowing more freedom of the press.

Perestroika involved a rethinking of some of the Soviet Union's long-cherished economic tenets, including the prohibition on private enterprise. Gorbachev also supported a new treaty of union that would end Moscow's and the CPSU's centralized hold on the individual republics, instead creating a new federation of independent republics, but just prior to its signing in August 1991 Gorbachev was surprised by a delegation of top-ranking officials at his summer home in the Crimea. They included the country's ministers for defense and the interior as well as the head of the KGB [committee for state security], and he was kept under house arrest while a coup [takeover of power] attempt was made at the seat of government in Moscow's Kremlin. Large public demonstrations erupted in both Moscow and St. Petersburg, spurred in part by similar regime changes instigated in the Eastern European countries two years earlier thanks to popular pro-democracy uprisings that were genuine "people's revolutions," and the August 1991 coup came to a quick and relatively bloodless end three days after it began. A provision of the Soviet constitution allowed republics to vote to secede from the Soviet Union, and each of their respective legislatures—with freely elected non-CPSU members now—took advantage of the clause and declared their independence.

A Dramatic End and a New Beginning

The August 1991 coup led to the outlawing of the CPSU, and Gorbachev resigned from office on December 25, 1991. That same month, the Commonwealth of Independent States was established by the former Soviet republics of Russia, Ukraine, and Belarus. A dramatic period of transformation began, with formerly state-owned companies sold off to private investors, who became wealthy almost overnight. Ordinary citizens, however, suffered tremendous hardships due to the end of the Soviet planned economy, which had regulated the price of food and housing. By the end of the decade, a former CPSU member and KGB officer, Vladimir Putin, had risen to power as president of the Russian Federation, and his domestic policies were criticized for appearing to rescind some of the democratic freedoms in place since the end of the Soviet Union.

Despite its rather spectacular collapse and dramatic end, the Soviet Union existed for a seventy-year period as one of the most important social and political experiments in the history of world government. The stated goals of the 1917 Revolution—the establishment of a classless and stateless communist society—never materialized, but the control of the CPSU over a population of 293 million Soviet citizens across 8.6 million square miles was unprecedented in human history, as was Moscow's management of the largest centrally planned economy in the world.

Legacy of the Soviet Union

As one of the two world superpowers for much of the twentieth century, the Soviet Union played a decisive role in nearly all major world events and social developments. . . . Soviet influence on the political life of Eastern Europe remained a difficult legacy even more than a decade after the collapse of the Berlin Wall and the end of the Soviet Bloc, as each of the newly independent nations struggled to join an international community of democratic, free-market states. Within the former constituent republics of the Soviet Union, too, governments strained to achieve a multiparty political life. . . .

What may be the Soviet Union's greatest legacy was the rapid transformation of a largely agrarian, near-medieval society into one of the most heavily industrialized, literate, and scientifically advanced nations in the world within just a few short decades—an achievement accomplished by the sheer force and power of a party leadership who recognized that their authority and the security of their state was dependent entirely on economic might, not ideological right.

A Coup Lives and Dies

Voice of America

In this August 15, 2001, Voice of America radio broadcast, an expert contends that Soviet president Mikhail Gorbachev's lack of popularity did not trigger the August 1991 coup in Russia intending to take control of the country away from him. The trigger was a proposed union treaty with the Soviet republics, which, if passed, would have taken away much of the power of the Soviet government. Gorbachev refused to believe there was a coup against him despite warnings to the contrary. The coup took place, but failed. Coup leaders lacked resolve and were not willing to use force or take other measures that would have made the coup a success. Voice of America is the official broadcasting service of the U.S. government.

On August 18, 1991, eight high-ranking Soviet officials placed Soviet President Mikhail Gorbachev under house arrest and took control of the government of the USSR. Less than 72 hours later, their coup had collapsed, but it would change the course of history

SOURCE. "Proposed Union Treaty Triggered 1991 Soviet Coup, Expert Says," VOAnews.com, August 15, 2001. Reproduced by permission.

in a way that no one—certainly not the plotters themselves—could have foreseen.

The reports on Echo Moskvy radio that tanks were in the streets of the capital were a shock for the citizens of Moscow. But as dramatic as the news was that an "emergency committee" had taken power, it was not a surprise.

For months it was clear that many in the Soviet leadership were unhappy with Mikhail Gorbachev's reforms, which they believed were causing the Soviet Union to unravel.

> It was not Mr. Gorbachev's lack of popularity that triggered the coup. The deciding factor was the coming union treaty with the country's republics.

Gorbachev Disregards Warning About a Coup

During August 1991, Mr. Gorbachev was putting the final touches on a new union treaty that would give even greater independence to the Soviet states. Lithuania had already declared independence and more Soviet states were following suit. That some inside the leadership wanted to turn back the clock was no surprise. "Everyone suspected that something is going to happen," says Yevgeny Volk who worked for the Supreme Soviet of the Russian Federation, an organization he describes as the headquarters of the anti-communist movement at the time. "Moscow Mayor Gavril Papov received information about it and shared it with [Russian president] Boris Yeltsin in late July," Mr. Volk says. "And, he called U.S. Ambassador [Jack] Matlock. Matlock wired a secret cable to President [George H.W.] Bush and President Bush called Gorbachev saying that 'you know there is a coup against you.' And Gorbachev said, 'I do not believe it.'"

Even though he had led a wave of unprecedented changes hailed around the world, by 1991 Mr. Gorbachev's popularity at home had nearly vanished. After five years

The role of Boris Yeltsin (left, holding papers) in ending the August 1991 coup against Soviet president Mikhail Gorbachev brought him to prominence that year. (**AP Images.**)

of promises, reforms failed to bring any real improvement in living standards.

But it was not Mr. Gorbachev's lack of popularity that triggered the coup. The deciding factor was the coming union treaty with the country's republics that would have taken away much of Soviet government's power by creating a confederation.

If Mr. Gorbachev did not believe a coup was in the offing, many others did, including Sergei Bradchikov, a businessman with no direct involvement in politics, but a strong belief in democracy. "I heard about it from my friends," he says. "They warned me in February [1991] that something would happen in August. So I knew it was coming, but I did not expect it to happen the way it did."

Profile: Boris Nikolaevich Yeltsin

Boris Nikolaevich Yeltsin was born February 1, 1931, in Siberia. . . . Shortly after he received an engineering degree from Ural Polytechnic Institute in 1955, he married fellow engineer Naina Girina. . . .

After working in construction he joined the Communist Party of the Soviet Union in 1961, and rose through the local party ranks. Selected to serve as the mayor of Moscow in the mid-1980s, he promoted reform but was forced to resign after criticizing party leaders. In March 1989 he was elected to the new Congress of People's Deputies and became the speaker of the Congress in May 1990.

During the August 1991 attempted coup, his popular support grew when he climbed onto an advancing tank to address the army. After the coup failed, Yeltsin renounced the Communist Party of the Soviet Union and won Russia's first democratic presidential election. Although his first term was marked by the breakup of the Soviet Union, economic recession, internal strife, and a heart attack, he was reelected in July 1996. During his second term, tensions in Chechnya increased, and Yeltsin's health continued to suffer. . . . Yeltsin resigned as president on December 31, 1999. He died of heart failure April 23, 2007, in Moscow.

SOURCE: *"Boris Nikolaevich Yeltsin,"* History Behind the Headlines: The Origins of Conflicts Worldwide, *vol. 1. Farmington Hills, MI: Gale, 2001.*

Boris Yeltsin Takes a Stand

Sergei Bradchikov was also not expecting to be out in the street in front of the Russian White House—the seat of the Russian Federation's administration—part of a human shield that squared off against Soviet tanks. But that is where he found himself. He did it, he says, in defense of democracy. "I was not defending Boris Yeltsin personally or anybody else," he says. "I was fighting against the regime we had, for some democratic changes and reforms."

As courageous as Mr. Bradchikov and the other defenders were, it was clear from the beginning that the coup leaders lacked resolve. None of their key opponents were ever arrested.

Mikhail Gorbachev's phone lines at his dacha [country house] in Crimea had been cut, but Boris Yeltsin was receiving calls from around the world, and even ordered food from Moscow's Pizza Hut. Mr. Yeltsin even phoned the Emergency Committee, as the coup leaders called themselves, denouncing them [as] a "gang of bandits."

> In the end, the coup leaders' attempt to roll back the clock only hastened the end of the system they wanted to preserve.

Mr. Yeltsin appeared outside the White House [a government building in Moscow] where he scrambled aboard a tank in front of 20,000 protesters and called for mass resistance.

Boris Yeltsin denounced the coup as unconstitutional and called for a general strike, declaring himself the "Guardian of Democracy."

Fear of Using Force Leads to Failure

The crowds began to grow. Veterans of the Afghanistan war [a war between anticommunist Muslims and Soviet forces lasting from 1979–1988] set up barricades in front of the White House and made Molotov cocktails [bombs]. The building was surrounded by people from all walks of Russian life, from students and defecting soldiers to priests and pensioners.

By the end of the day on August 19, troops were going over to Mr. Yeltsin's side, and many of the elite commando divisions were now protecting the White House.

Even though the Emergency Committee imposed a curfew on Moscow the next day, no one paid attention to it. Crowds started to raise the old white, blue, and red Russian flag. Famed cellist Mistislav Rostropovich even flew in from Paris for an impromptu concert.

Yeltsin supporter Yevgeny Volk said that from the beginning the Emergency Committee lacked the will to take firm measures to ensure the coup's success. "They were afraid of using force," Volk says. "They understood that their prestige in the international community would be ruined after a military suppression of the democracy and pro-reform forces here. That is why they were always hesitant. They never decided to storm the White House."

In the end, the coup leaders' attempt to roll back the clock only hastened the end of the system they wanted to preserve. Although official dissolution of the Soviet Union would not take place until December 25, 1991, after August 22 the USSR existed in name only.

Russia, Ukraine, and Belorussia Declare the Soviet Union Dissolved

Michael Dobbs

In the following viewpoint published December 9, 1991, *Washington Post* correspondent Michael Dobbs reports on the formal announcement by the three Slavic republics of Russia, Ukraine, and Belorussia [now Belarus] that the Soviet Union has been dissolved and that they have agreed to establish in its place a new entity—a Commonwealth of Independent States. Dobbs contends that the move by the republics will have broad constitutional repercussions and probably will put added pressure on Western governments to deal with individual republics instead of the central government. Michael Dobbs is a reporter for the *Washington Post* and has spent much of his career as a foreign correspondent covering the collapse of communism. His

1997 work *Down with Big Brother: The Fall of the Soviet Empire* was a runner-up for the 1997 PEN literary award for nonfiction.

The leaders of Russia, the Ukraine and Byelorussia [now Belarus] formally announced the dissolution of the Soviet Union today [December 8, 1991] and said they had agreed to establish a "Commonwealth of Independent States" in its place.

The decision to liquidate the 69-year-old Communist-forged union and halt activity of all Soviet government organs came during a closed-door meeting at a Byelorussian hunting lodge near the Polish border in the absence of Soviet President Mikhail Gorbachev.

> 'As founding states of the U.S.S.R. . . . we declare that the U.S.S.R. is ceasing its existence as a subject of international law and a geopolitical reality.'

Reactions and Implications

There was no immediate comment from Gorbachev, whose constitutional position as president and commander in chief of the 4-million-member Soviet armed forces has now been challenged throughout the Slavic heartland of the former Soviet superpower.

In Washington, Secretary of State James A. Baker III said in a television interview that "the Soviet Union as we've known it no longer exists," but he warned that there is still a risk of civil war amid the ruins of the Soviet empire.

In a joint communique at the end of a two-day Slavic summit, the three leaders declared: "As founding states of the U.S.S.R. . . . we declare that the U.S.S.R. is ceasing its existence as a subject of international law and a geopolitical reality." The three also agreed to establish unified control over the Soviet Union's 27,000 nuclear warheads and coordinate foreign relations and economic

The heads of Russia (Boris Yeltsin, left), Ukraine (Leonid Kravchuk), and Belorussia (Stanislav Shuskevitch, not shown) announced the dissolution of the USSR on December 8, 1991. (**AP Images.**)

activity, but they offered no details about how this was to be accomplished.

The dramatic move by the three republics, which account for 70 percent of the Soviet Union's 290 million population and 80 percent of its industrial output, has far-reaching constitutional implications that are likely to take some time to unfold.

It is also likely to increase the political pressure on Western governments to deal with individual republics rather than the central government, and a White House spokesman said Russian President Boris Yeltsin discussed the new commonwealth with [U.S.] President [George H.W.] Bush today in a 30-minute telephone conversation.

> '1 [Mikhail Gorbachev] am the center. This is the current situation and the situation that will remain.'

The New Reality: Independent States

The three republics claimed the right to dissolve the Soviet Union as co-signatories of the 1922 treaty that established it, but this could still be disputed by Gorbachev or by the other republics. The communique invites all other former Soviet republics to join the commonwealth, which will have its headquarters in Minsk, the capital of Byelorussia, rather than Moscow, the historic Russian capital.

The declaration was signed by Yeltsin, Ukrainian President Leonid Kravchuk and Byelorussian parliamentary chairman Stanislav Shuskevitch after two days of talks in Viskuoi, near the Byelorussian city of Brest. All three men are due in Moscow Monday [December 9] to present Gorbachev and Kazakhstan President Nursultan Nazarbayev—the most influential of the non-Slavic Soviet leaders—with what amounts to a fait accompli [accomplished fact].

The statement by the three Slavic leaders said that lengthy negotiations chaired by Gorbachev on a modified union of former Soviet republics had reached an impasse and that the establishment of independent states on former Soviet territory had become a "reality." It accused the Soviet authorities of pursuing "a shortsighted policy" that had led the country into a deep economic and political crisis.

Born out of the turmoil of the 1917 Bolshevik Revolution and a brutal civil war involving Communists, monarchists and various nationalist forces, the Soviet

Union came into existence formally on Dec. 30, 1922. It eventually expanded to occupy one-sixth of the Earth's surface, gobbling up the Baltic states of Lithuania, Latvia and Estonia during World War II, as well as sizable chunks of prewar Poland and Romania.

Gorbachev and the Ukraine

Over the past few days, Gorbachev has stepped up his warnings of "catastrophe" and "anarchy" if the former Soviet republics did not agree to some form of political union, and in an interview on French television broadcast earlier today, he said that the disintegration of the Soviet Union would make the civil war in Yugoslavia look like "a joke."

"I am the center. This is the current situation and the situation that will remain," Gorbachev told the interviewer in response to a question about control of nuclear weapons, which currently are located in the three Slavic republics and Kazakhstan.

Tonight [December 8], Ukrainian television broadcast a recorded interview with Gorbachev in which the Soviet leader pounded his fist on a table and pledged to do everything in his power to keep the Ukraine, with its 53 million inhabitants, in the union. The Ukrainian interviewer accused him of wanting to turn back the "wheel of history" and failing to understand Ukrainian aspirations for independent statehood after being under Russian domination for more than 300 years.

Although the agreement to create the Commonwealth of Independent States liquidates the present central government, as personified by Gorbachev, it meets at least some of the longstanding goals of the 61-year-old Soviet president. It speaks of "a unified command of a common military-strategic space," coordination of foreign policy among member states, common transportation and communication systems, and a common economic and customs union.

Respect for Territorial Integrity: A Hallmark of the New Commonwealth

The principal difference between the new Commonwealth of Independent States and the "Confederation of Sovereign States" advocated by Gorbachev lies in the relationship between a central political structure and the republics. The Russian term *sodruzhestvo*, which can be translated as either commonwealth or community, clearly envisages a looser form of association than confederation or federation, with ultimate power vested in the individual member states.

The determination of Yeltsin and the other republic leaders to put an end to centuries of highly centralized rule was symbolized by the choice of the provincial city of Minsk as the headquarters for the commonwealth. The nearest equivalent is the role of Brussels as the focus of the European Community, which in many ways is a model for the kind of political association the Slavic leaders are seeking to achieve.

In an apparent attempt to defuse the politically sensitive issue of minority populations, the signatories of today's agreement promised to respect each other's territorial integrity and the "inviolability of existing borders." After the abortive Kremlin coup by hard-line Communists last August, Yeltsin provoked a major row with the Ukraine by suggesting that he might lay claim to Ukrainian lands in which ethnic Russians are in the majority.

While the coup fatally undermined Gorbachev's attempts to preserve a strong central authority, the death blow to the Soviet Union was dealt by an overwhelming vote in favor of Ukrainian independence from Moscow in a referendum two weeks ago. The 90 percent "yes" vote appears to have persuaded Yeltsin that

> The death blow to the Soviet Union was dealt by an overwhelming vote in favor of Ukrainian independence from Moscow.

Gorbachev's attempts to negotiate a new union treaty were doomed.

Economics and Armies

In a separate economic agreement, the three Slavic republics agreed to coordinate radical economic reforms aimed at creating a free-market system and free enterprise in place of Communist central planning. The Russian government announced late last week that it will lift price controls from most goods beginning Dec. 16, [1991,] forcing other republics to follow suit if they wish to prevent a mass shift of available food and consumer goods to Russian territory.

The republic leaders agreed to use the Russian ruble to settle accounts among commonwealth members and to sign an inter-bank agreement aimed at regaining control over the chaotic money supply. They fixed a 10-day deadline for coordinating common defense expenditures for next year and for funding continuing cleanup efforts stemming from the 1986 Chernobyl nuclear disaster, whose deadliest impact was in the Ukraine and Byelorussia.

While the agreement speaks of joint control over nuclear weapons, it does not exclude the establishment of individual national armies. The Ukraine has already announced plans for a 450,000-member army, while Russia is forming a national guard.

The dominant Soviet republic has a population of 147.4 million and controls most of the Soviet Union's natural resources. It stretches across the entire Eurasian land mass, from the Baltic Sea to the Sea of Japan.

President Boris Yeltsin's administration steadily has taken power from the central government since the August coup. But Russia faces many internal problems, including high inflation, food shortages and secessionist movements in ethnic regions such as Tatarstan and Chechen-Ingush.

Mikhail Gorbachev Resigns as President of the Soviet Union

Daniel Sneider

In the following newspaper article from December 26, 1991, Daniel Sneider reports on Mikhail Gorbachev's resignation as president of the Soviet Union and on his accomplishments and failures. Gorbachev was called in to renovate a decaying system and save the Soviet Union. He instituted major reforms intended to transform the economy and the entire system of social relations and bring about democratization. In spite of Communist Party resistance to and rejection of his efforts and reforms, Gorbachev made some headway. In the end, however, his reforms reached their limit and Gorbachev gave in to pressure. The rise to the forefront of Boris Yeltsin and Gorbachev's loss of power to new nationalist movements served to hasten his fall from power. Daniel Sneider is a staff writer for the *Christian Science Monitor*.

SOURCE. Daniel Sneider, "December 25, 1991: Gorbachev Resigns as President of the Soviet Union," *Christian Science Monitor*, December 26, 1991. Copyright © 1991 The Christian Science Publishing Society. All rights reserved. Reproduced by permission from *Christian Science Monitor* (www.csmonitor.com).

> 'Gorbachev took this country like my wife takes cabbage.'

With sadness, anger, and flashes of defiance, Mikhail Sergeyevich Gorbachev ends a momentous six and a half years at the helm of his nation.

A Futile Effort

The West sees Mr. Gorbachev as a singular figure. But in his role as unrequited Russian reformer, Gorbachev has trod a well-worn path. From Czar Alexander II to Nikita Khrushchev, leaders before him have broken their swords battling to prod the vast country forward. They all met with what history has revealed to be the futility of trying to save a dying system through reform.

"During my tenure, I have been attacked by all those in Russian society who can scream and write. . . . The revolutionaries curse me because I have strongly and conscientiously favored the use of the most decisive measures. . . . As for the conservatives, they attack me because they have mistakenly blamed me for all the changes in our political system."

These words could have been written by Gorbachev—indeed he said as much many times. But they were penned by another great Russian reformer, Count Sergei Iulevich Witte, in his bitter resignation letter as prime minister in 1906. Witte had saved Nicholas II and his autocracy from war and revolution, only to be discarded.

The Goal: Mend a Decaying System

Like Witte, Gorbachev was called in to save a society in collapse. The Russian empire was again weakened by foreign adventures, culminating in the disastrous war in Afghanistan. And underneath, the economic system was decaying, unable to meet basic needs.

"Gorbachev took this country like my wife takes cabbage. He thought that to get rid of the dirt, he could just peel off the top layer of leaves. But he had to keep going until there was nothing left." That is the assessment of Vitaly Korotich, who was Gorbachev's designated spearhead in the campaign to reclaim lost history as editor of the magazine *Ogonyok*.

Even before he took office as general secretary of the Communist Party of the Soviet Union (CPSU) in March 1985, Gorbachev described his goal as the renovation of the socialist system. In a speech on Dec. 10, 1984, he delivered his later famous watchwords: deep transformations in the economy and the whole system of social relations, "perestroika (restructuring) of economic management, democratization of our social and economic life," and "glasnost" (openness).

Gorbachev reduced fear in Soviet society and let a fresh wind blow through Eastern Europe. But when those reforms reached their limits— and they did so quickly—Gorbachev balked. The ultimate assault on the Leninist state and its state-run economy was always beyond his intent.

> 'Gorbachev did not have a clear plan of what kind of political and social system must be created.'

Following Yuri Andropov's Path

In much of this Gorbachev was following a path laid out by his political sponsor, Yuri Andropov, who advanced from chairman of the KGB [Committee for State Security] to succeed Leonid Brezhnev as party leader in 1982. Andropov was described by those around him as a closet liberal, a lover of jazz who sought to bring socialist democracy to the Soviet Union. But Andropov died in early 1984. Gorbachev had to wait more than a year until the Brezhnev protégé, conservative stalwart Konstantin Chernenko, came and went in similar fashion.

Gorbachev began with familiar themes of Andropov: the need to restore discipline, to intensify production through technological progress and innovations such as giving state-run enterprises more freedom and workers salary incentives. These moves picked up the reformist thread of Khrushchev, lost during the long years under Brezhnev, which Gorbachev disdainfully referred to as "the era of stagnation."

"Gorbachev did not have a clear plan of what kind of political and social system must be created," says Fyodor Burlatsky, a former speechwriter for Khrushchev, close aide to Andropov, and sometime adviser to Gorbachev. "He came from our generation, from the 60s. He had in mind what Khrushchev wanted but maybe more than Khrushchev. He shared the . . . feeling that everything that came from the Stalinist system must be destroyed. It doesn't mean that the socialist system must disappear."

Perhaps Gorbachev's clearest goal, Mr. Burlatsky suggests, was to improve relations with the West. Alone among Soviet leaders, Gorbachev had traveled extensively in the West. "He saw the terrible distance between our country and the Western countries. . . . He understood the West is more successful, but he did not understand the reason."

Party Resistance and Rejection

Among the small number of reformers Gorbachev gathered around himself was Alexander Yakovlev, a party intellectual whom Gorbachev rescued in 1983 from a 10-year semi-exile as ambassador to Canada. Mr. Yakovlev became the theorist of perestroika. Earlier this month [December 1991], in a little reported speech to the founding conference of the Movement for Democratic Reforms, Yakovlev reviewed the effort to reform Soviet communism.

"While the system completely rejected any attempt at sensible reform, Stalinist obstructions could be crushed only by a powerful ram. Khrushchev's direct and brave attack ended in defeat, although Brezhnev's refurbishing failed as well. A time of uncertainty settled in, but the outcome was already near and it came in the form of perestroika, elite revolution meant to develop in a peaceful way. Perhaps it couldn't have been otherwise. It was born within the politically active part of the CPSU and the society, and it was here that it encountered the most fierce resistance and rejection," he said.

In a rambling, nostalgic, two-hour farewell session with Soviet reporters on Dec. 12, Gorbachev still defended the attempt to bring reform via the party. "Under us everything was already boiling, starting with the 60s. All those attempts to begin the reforms were stifled. All those attempts mean that the problems had been knocking at the doors of our society for a long time already. . . . It was in the party where the forces were born that had the courage to decisively start the reforms. They took upon themselves the heaviest burden of responsibility."

For the first three years of his leadership, Gorbachev pursued his reforms in a series of thrusts, retreating slightly and advancing again on another front as each one met the opposition of Communist Party conservatives. By June 1988, when the 19th Party Conference dedicated to political reform was held, "the revolution from above . . . was at a crossroad," Yakovlev says.

> " Gorbachev faced a choice: to turn perestroika into . . . 'a truly, people's democratic revolution,' . . . or to remain a Communist reformer. "

Debate over the Kind of Democratic System to Create

At that moment, Gorbachev faced a choice: to turn perestroika into what Yakovlev calls "a truly, people's democratic revolution, going to the utmost, really bringing the society total freedom," or to remain a Communist reformer, operating in the familiar and controlled milieu of the party bureaucracy.

The path through the party was fraught with danger, Yakovlev says. Perestroika could "either be defeated

Mikhail Gorbachev delivers his resignation speech as the Soviet Union's last president on December 25, 1991. (**AP Images.**)

by Stalinist reaction, Brezhnevist conservatism, or risk being stolen from itself by those forces who just shield themselves with its slogans, striving in the meantime to redistribute power in the framework of the former social system."

In early 1988, a major debate was under way over what kind of democratic system should be created. Burlatsky was a member of a small working group under

Profile: Mikhail Sergeyevich Gorbachev

Mikhail Sergeyevich Gorbachev was born March 2, 1931, in Privolye, Russia, and spent most of his young life working on farms. He received his law degree in 1955; the next year he married Raisa Titorenka.

Gorbachev continued his education and graduated as an agronomist-economist. He became the youngest member of the Politburo (the policy-making body of the USSR), in 1980. He became head of state on March 11, 1985, when elected general secretary of the Communist Party.

Gorbachev's original goals were soon eclipsed by more drastic reform policies such as *glasnost* (openness) and *perestroika* (restructuring). He signed a pact with the U.S. in 1987 to limit nuclear weapons, and was elected to retain the presidency by the newly created parliament in 1988. When non-Communist governments came to power in former Soviet-bloc countries, Gorbachev withdrew Soviet troops. He was awarded the Nobel Peace Prize in 1990.

After being held under house arrest in August 1991 during a brief coup attempt, Gorbachev quit the Communist Party. On December 25, 1991, Gorbachev resigned as the president of the Soviet Union, which subsequently ceased to exist. Although a 1996 re-election bid garnered less than one percent of the vote, Gorbachev continues to be involved in Russian politics and environmental and educational foundations. In 2009 he announced he is creating a new social-democratic political party in Russia, the "Independent Democratic Party of Russia."

SOURCE: *"Mikhail Sergeyevich Gorbachev,"* History Behind the Headlines: The Origins of Conflicts Worldwide, *vol. 1. Farmington Hills, MI: Gale, 2001.*

the direction of Gorbachev's long-time associate Anatoly Lukyanov, which included close aide and politician-scientist Georgi Shakhnazarov. Two proposals came from this group, according to Burlatsky: one of his own and one from Mr. Lukyanov.

Lukyanov proposed removing the Stalin-era system and going back to Lenin's 1924 Constitution. That structure was based on indirect, two-stage elections of a parliament, while concentrating legal authority in local soviets (councils), with a vague definition of the relation between the party and the soviets.

Some participants in this process claim the intent was always to introduce multiparty democracy, though carefully, with the party in control of the process. But Burlatsky says that when he proposed direct elections of parliament, president, and vice-president on a multiparty basis, he was strongly opposed by almost everybody except Yakovlev.

> 'I missed the moment,' Gorbachev said.

Gorbachev opted for the Lukyanov plan, carrying out a complex election in March 1989 in which some deputies were directly elected and others sent by official organizations. They in turn chose a relatively tame standing parliament. Even this opened the political process. The live broadcasts of the first session of the Congress, with the dramatic appearance of long-time dissident Andrei Sakharov, captivated the nation.

In the spring of 1990, Gorbachev again had an opportunity to overturn the political system. Article 6 of the Constitution giving the Communist Party a monopoly had been abolished and a presidential system was to be established. But he chose to be elected by the Congress instead of by the people. This was "his greatest political mistake," says Burlatsky. "Gorbachev is not like Khrushchev; he doesn't like risk."

"Perestroika didn't manage to overcome itself," Yakovlev explains. "Public, social, and political forces awakened by it remained unclaimed, while the old structures continued to exist and act against reforms."

The 500-Day Plan

But in a sense those forces were claimed, though not by Gorbachev. Perestroika brought another unforeseen, and for Gorbachev unhappy, result: the emergence of powerful nationalist movements in the 15 republics of the Soviet empire. From the Baltic republics to the heartland of Russia, democratic reformers won power by detaching themselves from the Communist Party.

Boris Yeltsin, the brash Urals party boss whom Gorbachev had brought to Moscow to lead reforms there, rode this wind. He was helped by the party conservatives who, with Gorbachev's consent, ousted Mr. Yeltsin from their leadership ranks in 1987. Yeltsin's comeback, culminating in his defeat of Gorbachev's choice for the post of chairman of the Russian parliament in June 1990, marked the second crossroad for Gorbachev.

Frustrated radical reformers quickly gathered around Yeltsin—men such as economist Grigory Yavlinsky whose plan for a quick 500-day march to a market economy had been buried by the plodding bureaucrats around Gorbachev. In August 1990, Gorbachev agreed to draft a new economic reform plan together with Yeltsin, based on the 500-day scheme, raising hopes that perestroika would finally breach the boundaries of the old system.

The party and state bureaucracy fought back, warning Gorbachev of collapse if such a radical course were pursued. Gorbachev cracked, coming out in October in favor of a deeply compromised, cautious approach.

"Since the autumn of 1990, the reactionaries and conservatives were launching open attacks," recounts Yakovlev. "I am convinced that the rejection of the 500-day plan served as an encouraging signal to them. It was a mistake with grave consequences. It demonstrated that perestroika was ready to retreat under pressure."

Gorbachev's Loss of Power

"I missed the moment," Gorbachev said in a newspaper interview this week. "I should have formed a strong alliance with democrats. . . . And in general I paid an enormous price."

In the months that followed, Gorbachev turned to the right, surrounding himself with foes of reform and losing the counsel of old friends such as Yakovlev and Foreign Minister Eduard Shevardnadze. "Thus the way was opened to bloodshed in Vilnius and to the putsch [secretly planned attempt to remove a government by force] dress rehearsal held in Moscow on March 28, 1991," says Yakovlev referring to the military crackdown in Lithuania in January 1991 and the display of military force in the streets of Moscow, part of an effort to oust Yeltsin from power.

In the end, it was Yeltsin who saved Gorbachev from the hard-liners who finally moved to overthrow him in August. But in the bargain, Gorbachev lost power to the new nationalist movements.

"The main goal of my life has been accomplished," Gorbachev reflected in his Kremlin talk with reporters. "All the rest . . . well, maybe someone else will come and do it better. But you must understand, I wanted to succeed. What's special about me is that I can't accept defeat."

Tracing the Collapse of the USSR

Jeremy Bransten

The following viewpoint, excerpted from Jeremy Bransten's 2001 report on the breakup of the Soviet Union for Radio Free Europe/Radio Liberty, details events in 1990 and 1991 that culminated in the declaration of independence by former Soviet republics, the collapse of the Soviet Union, the resignation of Soviet President Mikhail Gorbachev, and the death of communism in the Soviet Union. In 1990, the country was falling apart, threatened by revolts, general unrest, declarations of independence, shortages of basic essentials, and a rapidly falling economy. The final blows were dealt in 1991 with the unveiling of an unpopular draft union treaty, a failed attempt to take over the government, and a shift to Russian leadership spearheaded by Russian president Boris Yeltsin. Jeremy Bransten is a senior editor/correspondent for Radio Free Europe/Radio Liberty.

SOURCE. Jeremy Bransten, "USSR Breakup: Tracing the Collapse of the World's Last Great Empire (Part I)," *Radio Free Europe/Radio Liberty*, December 14, 2001. Reprinted with the permission of Radio Free Europe/Radio Liberty, 1201 Connecticut Ave., N.W., Washington DC 20036. www.rferl.org.

When he began his twin campaign of glasnost [openness] and perestroika [restructuring] in the late 1980s, Soviet leader Mikhail Gorbachev intended to reform the Soviet Union. But Gorbachev had not counted on the fact that greater freedom would fan the forces of nationalism, and he vastly underestimated the speed of the country's economic decay. . . .

Major Change and Growing Tensions

By 1990, Lithuania had declared independence. Armenia and Azerbaijan were at war over Nagorno-Karabakh [disputed region in Azerbaijan]. The Kremlin was linked to the brutal clampdown on revolts in Tbilisi, Riga, and Vilnius [capital cities in Soviet republics]. Shortages of basic household goods and foodstuffs were growing. At times, it felt as if Moscow was losing control.

> 'The whole country was falling apart before our very eyes and not because we were planning it.'

Former Ukrainian President Leonid Kravchuk, in an interview with RFE/RL [Radio Free Europe/Radio Liberty], recalled the atmosphere: "The whole country was falling apart before our very eyes and not because we were planning it. The Baltics had left the fold, the war in Armenia, Azerbaijan, the events in Tbilisi. The whole country was waiting in lines. The economy was plummeting, and we needed to find a way out."

In December 1990, Soviet Foreign Minister Eduard Shevardnadze abruptly resigned, warning of a creeping coup by those opposed to reforms.

The rest of the winter, into 1991, was lived in an atmosphere of escalating tension as the leader of the Russian republic, Boris Yeltsin, increased his rhetoric against central Soviet institutions amid discussions of a new union treaty to loosen the bonds of the USSR.

In leaving his post, Soviet Foreign Minister Eduard Shevardnadze warned in 1990 of a coming coup. (**Sasha Stone/Time Life Pictures/ Getty Images.**)

Hard-liners—as Shevardnadze predicted—spoke out with increasing agitation against what they saw as the country's dissolution. Gorbachev zigzagged in his policies, trying in vain to pick a middle course between the two camps.

On 8 March 1991, the Kremlin unveiled a draft union treaty. The document offered the republics greater sovereignty, granting them control of economic and cultural development, and allowing them to establish diplomatic ties, sign international treaties, and join international organizations. A new name for the country was to be discussed, excluding the words "Socialist" and "Soviet."

Despite the conciliatory language, six of the USSR's 15 republics chose to ignore a referendum on the issue. Undeterred, Gorbachev continued to work on the treaty.

The Beginning of the End for Mikhail Gorbachev

At the start of August, presidential adviser Aleksandr Yakovlev—called by some the "architect" of perestroika—resigned, warning his boss of the dangers of a coup. Before that, then-U.S. President George [H.W.] Bush had taken the unprecedented step of telephoning Gorbachev from Washington to warn him of the same. The Soviet president was unfazed, as he recalled in a 1996 interview with RFE/RL: "Bush phoned me, and I said: 'George, you can sleep soundly. Nothing's going to happen.' That's what I said."

On 4 August, Gorbachev left with his family for his annual vacation in the Crimea, intending to complete a new version of the union treaty. On 18 August, shortly before five in the afternoon, Gorbachev's chief of staff, accompanied by Politburo [executive committee] member Oleg Shenin and a small clutch of senior government officials, arrived at the presidential dacha [home]. They demanded that Gorbachev sign a decree declaring a state of emergency, or resign.

Gorbachev refused to do either. The officials confiscated the codes needed to launch the Soviet Union's nuclear weapons, the so-called "nuclear briefcase." Gorbachev and his family were, in effect, under house arrest.

Takeover by the State Committee on the State of Emergency

The next morning, on 19 August, the coup leaders went public. TASS news agency [the official news agency of Russia] carried an announcement that Gorbachev had been relieved of his duties for health reasons. His powers were assumed by Vice President Gennadii Yanayev. A State Committee on the State of Emergency (GKChP) was established, led by eight officials, including KGB [Committee for State Security] head Vladimir Kryuchkov, Soviet Prime Minister Valentin Pavlov, and Defense Minister Dmitry Yazov. All strikes and demonstrations were banned.

Soon, the "Gang of Eight," as they were later dubbed, appeared on television. Yanayev seemed especially nervous—or perhaps drunk. His hands shook. He told viewers that, due to illness, Gorbachev had been forced to give up his duties. Yanayev said he would be the country's acting president.

"Because of Mikhail Sergeevich Gorbachev's inability to perform his duties as the president of the USSR, due to health reasons, in accordance with Article 127 of the Constitution of the USSR, the vice president of the USSR has temporarily assumed the office of acting president."

Although he pledged that the GKChP would continue Gorbachev's policies, Yanayev said the disintegration of the USSR could not be allowed to proceed.

"In many regions of the USSR, as a result of ethnic conflicts, blood is being shed, and the disintegration of the USSR would have the most serious consequences, both domestic and international."

Denouncement and a Call for Mass Resistance

Later that morning, Russian President Boris Yeltsin and other key Russian politicians denounced the coup as unconstitutional and called for a general strike. A joint

> 'We believe, and believed, that these methods of force are unacceptable . . . [and] discredit the Soviet Union before the entire world.'

statement—by Yeltsin, Russian Prime Minister Ivan Silayev, and Ruslan Khasbulatov, who was to become chairman of the Supreme Soviet—was issued, condemning the motives of the coup-plotters.

"On the night of 18–19 August 1991, outside of the ruling power and the law, the president of the country was removed. No reasons can be given to justify this removal. This is a case of a right-wing, reactionary, anticonstitutional coup. We believe, and believed, that these methods of force are unacceptable. They discredit the Soviet Union before the entire world, damage our prestige in international society, and return us to the Cold War era and the isolation of the Soviet Union from the rest of the world."

Yeltsin told a news conference that the GKChP's orders would not be carried out in Russia. Demonstrators began gathering on Moscow's Manezh Square, outside the Kremlin.

At 1 P.M., Yeltsin climbed atop a tank outside parliament—known as the White House—and issued a call for mass resistance. Tanks took up positions on all the bridges in central Moscow. Movement on the capital's main Tverskaya Street was blocked by armored personnel carriers.

Moscow military commander Nikolai Smirnov said a state of emergency had been declared and that troops had been brought in to defend order and interdict "terrorist acts."

At 4:30 P.M., Moscow Deputy Mayor Yuri Luzhkov denounced the coup and called on citizens to heed Yeltsin's call for mass protests. A few minutes later, Yeltsin issued a decree declaring all USSR government bodies located on Russian territory, including the KGB, subordinate to his authority.

A Call for Allegiance to Boris Yeltsin

Demonstrators around the White House spent the afternoon building barricades in anticipation of an army assault. That evening, Russian Vice President Aleksandr Rutskoi, whose legendary military career made him a powerful spokesperson, urged his fellow soldiers to side with those fighting the coup.

His words were to take an ironic significance just two years later, when Rutskoi himself was arrested for participating in an armed uprising against Yeltsin, his former ally.

"Comrades, I am an officer of the Soviet Army, a colonel, a hero of the Soviet Union, vice president of the Russian Federation. I have walked through the fiery path of Afghanistan and seen the horrors of war. I call on you, my comrade officers, soldiers and sailors, do not take action against the people—against your fathers, mothers, brothers and sisters. I appeal to your honor, your reason and your heart. Today the fate of the country, the fate of its free and democratic development, is in your hands. I call on you to cross over to the side legally elected by the people, the organs of power, the president of the Russian Federation and the Council of Ministers of the Russian Federation of Soviet Socialist Republics."

> 'The initiative shifted fully to the Russian leadership, which had defended democracy and naturally felt itself to be in the saddle.'

That same evening, Leningrad Mayor Anatolii Sobchak called for a citywide strike to begin the next day. Across Russia, confusion reigned, as some officials publicly declared their allegiance to Yeltsin. Others adopted a wait-and-see attitude. The night passed without incident, amid mounting tension.

On 20 August, Yeltsin spoke by telephone with then-U.S. President Bush, who told him Washington would not recognize the Yanayev government. In the evening, with reports of tanks moving toward the White House, Yeltsin offered amnesty to all military personnel and police who switched their allegiances and ignored the GKChP's orders. . . .

Shortly after midnight on the morning of 21 August, a column of military vehicles approached the barricades around the White House. Clashes ensued. Two protesters attempting to block the vehicles' way were shot, a third was crushed under tank treads. Crowds swarmed the vehicles. One armored personnel carrier was set on fire. The others soon retreated. The coup had collapsed.

The Rebirth of Russia

The next day, the "Gang of Eight" was arrested. The statue of Felix Dzerzhinsky, founder of the secret police in 1917, was toppled in front of KGB headquarters in central Moscow. Gorbachev was free to return. But the crowds were chanting Yeltsin's name.

Yeltsin and the entire Russian leadership would not give up this chance. As Gorbachev himself noted, in his 1996 interview: "The initiative shifted fully to the Russian leadership, which had defended democracy and naturally felt itself to be in the saddle."

Yeltsin, speaking on 23 August 1991, called on an exuberant crowd of supporters to work for the rebirth of Russia.

"The people have already freed themselves from the fear which they harbored just a few years ago. I call on all my fellow citizens, in the name of unity, to get to work for the renewal and resurrection of Russia, to work for the victory of democracy over reactionary forces, so that things can be as they were in wthe times of [the early Russian state of] Rus'! Hurray!"

Within days, the USSR's republics would declare their independence, and by December, the USSR would formally cease to exist. Gorbachev resigned as a leader without a country. . . .

The dream and promise of Soviet founder Vladimir Lenin, made in 1918, was now consigned, ironically, to the ash heap of history:

"Soviet power, no matter what happens—to the supporters of communism in various countries—Soviet power is inescapable and in the near future will triumph across the world."

For a time during the 20th century, it appeared Lenin's prediction might have come close to being realized. But like all regimes and ideologies, Soviet communism had a limited lifespan.

The United States Welcomes the New Commonwealth of Independent States

George H.W. Bush

In this 1991 U.S. State Department dispatch, President George H.W. Bush gives recognition to the newly formed Commonwealth of Independent States and to the individual republics within the union. For more than forty years the United States led the struggle against communism. With the dissolution of the Soviet Union and the formation of the Commonwealth by former Soviet republics, the confrontation between the United States and the Soviet Union came to an end and democracy and freedom were deemed victorious. The new states were committed to building democratic and civil societies, and the United States was willing to work with them to uphold the peace and help them build a successful future. George Bush was the forty-first president of the United States.

SOURCE. George H.W. Bush, "U.S. Welcomes New Commonwealth of Independent States—former Soviet Union," US Department of State Dispatch, December 30, 1991.

Good evening, and Merry Christmas to all Americans across our great country. During these last few months, you and I have witnessed one of the greatest dramas of the 20th century—the historic and revolutionary transformation of a totalitarian dictatorship, the Soviet Union, and the liberation of its peoples. As we celebrate Christmas—this day of peace and hope—I thought we should take a few minutes to reflect on what these events mean for us as Americans.

> The United States applauds and supports the historic choice for freedom by the new States of the Commonwealth.

A Victory for Democracy and Freedom

For over 40 years, the United States led the West in the struggle against communism and the threat it posed to our most precious values. This struggle shaped the lives of all Americans. It forced all nations to live under the specter of nuclear destruction.

That confrontation is now over. The nuclear threat—while far from gone—is receding. Eastern Europe is free. The Soviet Union itself is no more. This is a victory for democracy and freedom. It's a victory for the moral force of our values. Every American can take pride in this victory, from the millions of men and women who have served our country in uniform to millions of Americans who supported their country and a strong defense under nine Presidents.

The New States of the Commonwealth

New, independent nations have emerged out of the wreckage of the Soviet empire. Last weekend, these former Republics formed a Commonwealth of Independent States. This act marks the end of the old Soviet Union, signified today by Mikhail Gorbachev's decision to resign as President.

I'd like to express, on behalf of the American people, my gratitude to Mikhail Gorbachev for years of sustained commitment to world peace, and for his intellect, vision, and courage. I spoke with Mikhail Gorbachev this morning. We reviewed the many accomplishments of the past few years and spoke of hope for the future.

Mikhail Gorbachev's revolutionary policies transformed the Soviet Union. His policies permitted the peoples of Russia and the other republics to cast aside decades of oppression and establish the foundations of freedom. His legacy guarantees him an honored place in history and provides a solid basis for the United States to work in equally constructive ways with his successors.

The United States applauds and supports the historic choice for freedom by the new States of the Commonwealth. We congratulate them on the peaceful and democratic path they have chosen, and for their careful attention to nuclear control and safety during this transition. Despite a potential for instability and chaos, these events clearly serve our national interest.

Steps to Maintain Peace and Build a Prosperous Future

We stand tonight before a new world of hope and possibilities for our children, a world we could not have contemplated a few years ago. The challenge for us now is to engage these new States in sustaining the peace and building a more prosperous future.

And so today, based on commitments and assurances given to us by some of these states, concerning nuclear safety, democracy, and free markets, I am announcing some important steps designed to begin this process.

First, the United States recognizes and welcomes the emergence of a free, independent, and democratic Russia, led by its courageous President, Boris

> "Our enemies have become our partners, committed to building democratic and civil societies."

Yeltsin. Our Embassy in Moscow will remain there as our Embassy to Russia. We will support Russia's assumption of the USSR's seat as a permanent member of the UN Security Council. I look forward to working closely with President Yeltsin in support of his efforts to bring democratic and market reform to Russia.

Second, the United States also recognizes the independence of Ukraine, Armenia, Kazakhstan, Belarus, and Kyrgyzstan—all states that have made specific commitments to us. We will move quickly to establish diplomatic relations with these states and build new ties to them. We will sponsor membership in the United Nations for those not already members.

Granting of U.S. Recognition and Support

Third, the United States also recognized today as independent states the remaining six former Soviet Republics—Moldava, Turkmenistan, Azerbaijan, Tadjikistan, Georgia, and Uzbekistan. We will establish diplomatic relations with them when we are satisfied that they have made commitments to responsible security policies and democratic principles, as have the other states we recognize today.

These dramatic events come at a time when Americans are also facing challenges here at home. I know that for many of you, these are difficult times. And I want all Americans to know that I am committed to attacking our economic problems at home with the same determination we brought to winning the Cold War.

I am confident we will meet this challenge as we have so many times before. But we cannot if we retreat into isolationism. We will only succeed in this interconnected world by continuing to lead the fight for free people and free and fair trade. A free and prosperous global economy is essential for America's prosperity; that means jobs and economic growth right here at home.

Photo on previous page: U.S. President George H.W. Bush recognized the commonwealth of states that arose in the wake of the USSR's collapse. (AP Images.)

This is a day of great hope for all Americans. Our enemies have become our partners, committed to building democratic and civil societies. They ask for our support, and we will give it to them. We will do it because as Americans we can do no less.

For our children, we must offer them the guarantee of a peaceful and prosperous future—a future grounded in a world built on strong democratic principles, free from the specter of global conflict.

May God bless the people of the new nations in the Commonwealth of Independent States. And on this special day of peace on earth, good will toward men, may God continue to bless the United States of America.

CHAPTER 2

Controversies Surrounding the Dissolution of the Soviet Union

Perestroika Failed as a Program of Economic Restructuring

Peter J. Boettke

In the following viewpoint, Peter J. Boettke argues that Soviet President Mikhail Gorbachev's policy of perestroika (restructuring) failed completely as a program of economic restructuring. It did so primarily because none of the 10 programs Gorbachev introduced to drastically restructure the economy was implemented. There was no way the inconsistent and half-measures that were taken could have produced the economic results Gorbachev wanted. Politics got in the way, dominating economics as an organizing principle and making true reform unattainable. Peter J. Boettke is an assistant professor of economics at New York University. He is the author of several books on the history, collapse, and transition from socialism in the former Soviet Union, including the 1990 work *The Political Economy of the Soviet Socialism*.

Photo on previous page: A statue of Vladimir Lenin, founder of the USSR, stands in the Kremlin's Palace of Congress in Moscow. (**AP Images.**)

W hen Mikhail Gorbachev came to power in 1985, he inherited a political and economic mess. The Novosibirsk report prepared by Soviet sociologist Tatyana Zaslavskaya, published in the West in the spring of 1984, already had revealed the deep structural problems confronting the Soviet leadership. The years of Communist rule had choked the economy—stifling innovation and destroying initiative—and produced political cynicism born of overt corruption of the ruling elite. Gorbachev knew full well the extent of the situation he inherited.

Failure as a Result of Half-Measures and No Implementation

But after six years in power and despite much talk about renewal and restructuring, the economy is worse off and the Soviet Union no longer exists as a political entity. As a program of economic restructuring, perestroika must be judged as an utter failure. Glasnost [openness] to be sure produced a political and cultural awakening of sorts unknown during the 74 years of Communist rule, but perestroika failed to deliver the economic goods. Why?

One of the main reasons perestroika failed was because it wasn't tried. During his six years in power, Gorbachev introduced at least 10 programs for the "radical restructuring" of the Soviet economy, not a one of which was implemented. Instead, economic reform was limited to inconsistent and incoherent half-measures. The law on individual economic activity, the law on state enterprises, and the various price-reform proposals, for example, amounted to nothing more than half-measures incapable of producing the desired economic results even if they were implemented in an ideal environment.

The Logic of Politics

Conceptually, economic reform is a fairly simple matter. Private property in resources must be established and protected by a rule of law; consumer and producer subsidies must be eliminated; prices must be freed to adjust to the forces of supply and demand; responsible fiscal policy should be pursued that keeps taxation to a minimum and reins in deficit financing; and a sound currency must be established. Introducing such reforms . . . is anything but simple. And the major problem is not just a conceptual one of designing the appropriate sequence or plan of reform.

> "When politics is allowed to dominate economics as an organizing principle, political and economic irrationality result."

One of the most important insights derived from academic research in modern political economy is the potential conflict between good economics and good politics. In democratic regimes, where politicians depend on votes and campaign contributions to remain in office, research has shown that the logic of politics produces a shortsightedness with regard to economic policy. Popular economic policies are those that tend to yield short-term and easily identifiable benefits at the expense of long-term and largely hidden costs. Deficit financing and inflationary monetary policy are but two examples from Western economies.

In the formerly Communist political economies, this argument about the logic of politics can be intensified. The benefits of public policy fell mainly on the only constituency that mattered: the party bureaucracy. From the nice dacha [country home] to special access to stores, the party elite were the primary beneficiaries of the system. Economic reform promised to disrupt this system and yield very real short-term costs.

If market reforms had been introduced sincerely by Gorbachev, the short-term prospects would have been higher prices as consumer subsidies were eliminated, unemployment as inefficient state enterprises were shut down, and overt income inequality as new entrepreneurs

Sociologist Tatyana Zaslavskaya (left) prepared a key 1985 report on the troubled state of the USSR. (**AP Images.**)

took advantage of opportunities for economic profit. In other words, structural economic reform promised short-term and easily identifiable costs to be borne mainly by the party bureaucracy, and long-term and largely hidden benefits in terms of increased economic efficiency and consumer well-being. The logic of reform was in direct conflict with the logic of politics, and politics won out.

Economic Reality

Even though the ruling elite fought economic reform at every step, they could not repudiate economic reality. The Soviet economy had exhausted its accumulated surplus in terms of natural resources and Western technology and was unable to continue to develop. The economic situation grew worse under Gorbachev, and the demands for structural reform grew louder and more threatening to the old system. Glasnost, in addition to the events of

1989—from Tiananmen Square [in Beijing, China] to the Berlin Wall—mobilized the intellectual and cultural elite. As a Russian saying went, "We are still on the leash and the dog dish is still too far away, but now we can bark as loud as we want."

The failed August 1991 coup was the last gasp of the main beneficiaries of Soviet rule: the privileged apparatchiks [persons occupied full time by the Communist Party] and ruling elite. For 60 hours the world first shuddered, then gasped as the coup unraveled, and finally cheered as the ordeal ended. But the coup was a precondition for the beginning of real reform of the system. Otherwise, the party bureaucracy would still have held a degree of legitimacy and power that no longer exists. The displacement of dominant interest groups . . . is a prerequisite for systemic political and economic reform. . . .

As the leaders of the former Soviet republics debate their future economic and political ties and the legal frameworks that will govern their societies, they must bear in mind the most important lesson of the 74-year history of Soviet Communism—when politics is allowed to dominate economics as an organizing principle, political and economic irrationality result.

A workable constitution must protect against unwarranted political intrusions (even in the name of democracy) into the operation of economic forces. The law must establish "rules of the game" that protect the economic freedom of the people. Only in this manner can hope and prosperity come to a people who have been blessed with natural resources, but who have lived with the curse—first under the czars and then under the Communists—of bad rules that failed to restrain the political whims of the ruling elite.

Perestroika Was Not a Total Failure

Mikhail Gorbachev

In the following viewpoint, Mikhail Gorbachev contends that perestroika (restructuring) was needed to normalize life and bring the Soviet Union and its people into the modern techno-logical age. Perestroika would help the Soviet Union change its entire social and political process. It was an evolutionary process, a process of reform. Perestroika helped lay the foun-dations for normal, democratic, and peaceful development of the Soviet Union and its transformation into a normal member of the world community. Mikhail Gorbachev served as the last general secretary of the Communist Party of the Soviet Union from 1986–1991 and Executive President of the Soviet Union from 1980–1991, during which time he introduced perestroika and glasnost (openness), reform policies that revolutionized the internal and external affairs of the Soviet Union. In 1990 he was awarded the Nobel Peace Prize for his foreign policy initiatives.

SOURCE. Mikhail Gorbachev, *Gorbachev: On My Country and the World*. New York: Columbia University Press, 2000. Copyright © 2000 Columbia University Press. All rights reserved. Reprinted with per-mission of the publisher.

Perestroika [restructuring] was born out of the realization that problems of internal development in our country were ripe, even overripe, for a solution. New approaches and types of action were needed to escape the downward spiral of crisis, to normalize life, and to make a breakthrough to qualitatively new frontiers. It can be said that to a certain extent perestroika was a result of a rethinking of the Soviet experience since October.

The vital need for change was dictated also by the following consideration. It was obvious that the whole world was entering a new stage of development—some call it the postindustrial age, some the information age. But the Soviet Union had not yet passed through the industrial stage. It was lagging further and further behind those processes that were making a renewal in the life of the world community possible. Not only was a leap forward in technology needed but fundamental change in the entire social and political process. . . .

Perestroika: An Era of Struggle

This transition turned out to be extremely difficult and complicated, more complicated than it had seemed to us at first. . . . The entire perestroika era was filled with struggles—concealed at first and then more open, more fully exposed to public view—between the forces for change and those who opposed it. . . .

The complexity of the struggle stemmed from the fact that in 1985 the entire society—politically, ideologically, and spiritually—was still in the thrall of old customs and traditions. . . . There was another factor. Destroying the old system would have been senseless if we did not simultaneously lay the foundations for a new life. And this was genuinely unexplored

> "The foundations of the totalitarian system were eliminated. Profound democratic changes were begun."

Mikhail Gorbachev was one of the architects of glasnost, a policy that in turn supported perestroika. (**AP Images.**)

territory. The six-year perestroika era was a time filled with searching and discovery, gains and losses, breakthroughs in thought and action, as well as mistakes and oversights. The attempted coup in August 1991 interrupted perestroika. After that there were many developments, but they were along different lines, following different intentions. Still, in the relatively short span of six years we succeeded in doing a great deal. . . .

Accomplishments of Perestroika

What specifically did we accomplish as a result of the stormy years of perestroika? The foundations of the totalitarian system were eliminated. Profound democratic changes were begun. Free general elections were held for the first time, allowing real choice. Freedom of the press and a multiparty system were guaranteed. Representative bodies of government were established, and the first steps toward a separation of powers were taken. Human rights (previously in our country these were only "so-called," reference to them invariably made only in scornful quotation marks) now became an unassailable principle. And freedom of conscience was also established.

Movement began toward a multistructured, or mixed, economy providing equality of rights among all forms of property. Economic freedom was made into law. The spirit of enterprise began to gain strength, and processes of privatization and the formation of joint stock companies got under way. Within the framework of our new land law, the peasantry was reborn and private farmers made their appearance. Millions of hectares of land were turned over to both rural and urban inhabitants. The first privately owned banks also came on the scene. The different nationalities and peoples were given the freedom to choose their own course of development. Searching for a democratic way to reform our multinational state, to transform it from a unitary state in practice into a national federation, we reached the threshold at which a new union treaty was to be signed, based on the recognition of the sovereignty of each republic along with the preservation of a common economic, social, and legal space

> Perestroika would have been simply impossible if there had not been a profound and critical reexamination not only of the problems confronting our country but a rethinking of all realities.

that was necessary for all, including a common defense establishment.

Reexamining All Realities

The changes within our country inevitably led to a shift in foreign policy. The new course of perestroika predetermined renunciation of stereotypes and the confrontational methods of the past. It allowed for a rethinking of the main parameters of state security and the ways to ensure it. . . .

In other words, the foundations were laid for normal, democratic, and peaceful development of our country and its transformation into a normal member of the world community.

These are the decisive results of perestroika. Today, however, looking back through the prism of the past few years and taking into account the general trends of world development today, it seems insufficient to register these as the only results. Today it is evidently of special interest to state not only *what* was done but also *how* and *why* perestroika was able to achieve its results. . . .

Above all, perestroika would have been simply impossible if there had not been a profound and critical reexamination not only of the problems confronting our country but a rethinking of all realities—both national and international.

Previous conceptions of the world and its developmental trends and, correspondingly, of our country's place and role in the world were based, as we have said, on dogmas deeply rooted in our ideology, which essentially did not permit us to pursue a realistic policy. These conceptions had to be shattered and fundamentally new views worked out regarding our country's development and the surrounding world.

This task turned out to be far from simple. We had to renounce beliefs that for decades had been considered irrefutable truths, to reexamine the very methods and principles of leadership and action, indeed to rethink our surroundings entirely on a scientific basis (and not according to schemes inherited from ideological biases).

The New Way of Thinking

The product of this effort was the new thinking, which became the basis for all policy—both foreign and domestic—during perestroika. The point of departure for the new thinking was an attempt to evaluate everything not from the viewpoint of narrow class interests or even national interests but from the broader perspective: that of giving priority to the interests of all humanity with consideration for the increasingly apparent wholeness of the world, the interdependence of all countries and peoples, the humanist values formed over centuries.

The practical work of perestroika was to renounce stereotypical ideological thinking and the dogmas of the past. This required a fresh view of the world and of ourselves with no preconceptions, taking into account the challenges of the present and the already evident trends of the future in the third millennium.

During perestroika, and often now as well, the initiators of perestroika have been criticized for the absence of a "clear plan" for change. The habit developed over decades of having an all-inclusive regimentation of life. . . .

All this was present in perestroika: a profound democratization of public life and a guarantee of freedom of social and political choice. These goals were proclaimed and frequently reaffirmed. This did not exclude but presupposed the necessity to change one's specific reference points at each stage as matters proceeded and to engage in a constant search for optimal solutions.

Peaceful Gradual Change

An extremely important conclusion follows from the experience of perestroika: Even in a society formed under totalitarian conditions, democratic change is possible by peaceful evolutionary means. . . . In its inner content perestroika of course was a revolution. But in its form it was an evolutionary process, a process of reform. . . .

In the course of implementing change we did not succeed in avoiding bloodshed altogether. But that was a consequence solely of resistance by the opponents of perestroika in the upper echelons of the nomenklatura [an elite group in the Soviet Union]. On the whole the change from one system to another took place peacefully and by evolutionary means. Our having chosen a policy course that was supported from below by the masses made this peaceful transition possible. And our policy of glasnost [openness] played a decisive role in mobilizing the masses and winning their support. . . .

> In short, without glasnost there would have been no perestroika.

From the very beginning of the changes our country's leadership assigned primary importance to open communication with the people, including direct disclosure in order to explain the new course. Without the citizens' understanding and support, without their participation, it would not have been possible to move from dead center. That is why we initiated the policies of perestroika and glasnost simultaneously.

The Important Role of Glasnost

Like perestroika itself, glasnost made its way with considerable difficulty. The nomenklatura on all levels, which regarded the strictest secrecy and protection of authorities from criticism from below as the holy of holies of the regime, opposed glasnost in every way they could. . . . Even among the most sincere supporters of perestroika, the tradition over many years of making everything a secret made itself felt. But it was precisely glasnost that awakened people from their social slumber, helped them overcome indifference and passivity and become aware of the stake they had in change and of its important implications for their lives. Glasnost helped us to explain and promote awareness of the new realities and the essence of our new political course. In short, without glasnost there would have been no perestroika. The question of the relation between ends and means is one of the key aspects of politics and of political activity. If the means do not correspond to the ends, or, still worse, if the means contradict the ends, this will lead to setbacks and failure. . . .

In essence, glasnost became the means for drawing people into political activity, for including them in the creation of a new life, and this, above all, corresponded to the essence of perestroika. Glasnost not only created conditions for implementing the intended reforms but also made it possible to overcome attempts to sabotage the policy of change.

We are indebted to glasnost for a profound psychological transformation in the public consciousness toward democracy, freedom, and the humanist values of civilization. . . .

Perestroika confirmed once again that the normal, democratic development of society rules out universal secrecy as a method of administration. Democratic development presupposes glasnost—that is, openness, freedom of information for all citizens, and freedom of expression by them of their political, religious, and other views and convictions, freedom of criticism in the fullest sense of the word.

Gorbachev's Reforms Caused the Breakup of the Soviet Union

Michael Dobbs

In the following viewpoint, Michael Dobbs asserts that Mikhail Gorbachev wanted to reform, modernize, and democratize the Soviet Union on a grand scale and in the process set in motion the chain of events that led to its disintegration and to the collapse of Soviet communism. It was a major mistake on Gorbachev's part to think that the Communist Party could reform itself. By staying loyal to the party, he contributed to his downfall. Another major mistake was his handling of the economy. He took a course of action that resulted in one of the most disastrous economic slides ever experienced by an industrialized society. Michael Dobbs is a former Moscow bureau chief of the *Washington Post* and a longtime correspondent in Eastern Europe. His book *Down with Big Brother: The Fall of the Soviet Empire* was a runner-up for the 1997 PEN literary award for nonfiction.

SOURCE. Michael Dobbs, *Down with Big Brother: The Fall of the Soviet Empire*. New York: Alfred A. Knopf, 1997. Copyright © 1996 by Michael Dobbs. Used by permission of Alfred A. Knopf, a division of Random House, Inc., and the author.

Of all the outstanding leaders of the twentieth century—Lenin, Mao, Stalin, Hitler, Roosevelt, Churchill—the last general secretary of the Soviet Communist Party was surely the most contradictory. His name will be associated with epoch-making developments that were the very opposite of his original intention. He was the Communist who dismantled communism, the reformer who was overtaken by his own reforms, the emperor who allowed the world's last great multinational empire to break apart. He wanted to lead the Soviet Union into the information age but was destined to preside over its downfall. He launched a revolution and ended up becoming one of its victims.

[Mikhail Sergeyevich] Gorbachev's most important contribution lay not so much in what he *did* as in what he *permitted* to happen, almost in spite of himself. If [U.S. President] Ronald Reagan was the Great Communicator, Gorbachev was the Great Facilitator. In contrast with the early Bolsheviks, who set out to create utopia by force, Gorbachev permitted history to resume its natural course. He sought not to change the course of history but to swim in its tide. Even after it had become clear where his revolution was leading, he did not draw back from the consequences of his own actions.

The High Cost of Loyalty

Gorbachev's mistakes, like his political vision, were mistakes on the grand scale. He clung to the illusion that the Communist Party was capable of reforming itself long after it had been hopelessly discredited. An enthusiastic proponent of elections for other people, he never submitted his own record to the judgment of the voters. A decisive moment occurred in 1989, when he rejected the idea of a direct election and allowed himself to

> Gorbachev did more to hasten the end of the 'evil empire' through his muddled economic policies than anything Reagan could possibly have devised.

be nominated for a bloc of uncontested seats in the new Soviet parliament. Up until that point he could probably have won a popular mandate—the economy had not yet started to unravel, and his prestige was still high—but he chose to show solidarity with his Politburo [political bureau] colleagues. His loyalty to the party cost him dearly during the final showdown with [Russian President Boris] Yeltsin, when he found himself without a reliable political weapon. He renounced the use of the machine gun but failed to secure the legitimacy of the ballot box. He was never able to answer satisfactorily [Soviet physicist and political dissident] Andrei Sakharov's question at the first Congress of People's Deputies, "Whose side are you on, Mikhail Sergeyevich?"

Flawed Economic Policies

The other major failure was his handling of the economy. Gorbachev did more to hasten the end of the "evil empire" through his muddled economic policies than anything Reagan could possibly have devised. The deficit in the state budget had risen from just over 3 percent when Gorbachev came to power to a staggering 30 to 50 percent by the time he stepped down. Things started going wrong almost from the moment he arrived in office. The disastrous antialcohol campaign of 1986–87 eliminated the single most effective source of government revenue. In order to plug the deficit, government presses worked overtime, churning out increasingly worthless paper rubles. Gorbachev compounded his mistake by refusing to liberalize prices, a course of action that led to chronic shortages of both consumer goods and industrial components. This was the beginning of one of the most catastrophic economic slides ever experienced by an industrialized society.

> " History will record that it was Gorbachev who set in motion the chain of events that led to the disintegration of the world's first socialist state. "

Photo on previous page: Just as Ronald Reagan (right) was called "the Great Communicator," author Michael Dobbs calls Mikhail Gorbachev (left) "the Great Facilitator." (AP Images.)

Destruction from Within

These were monumental errors, but they served a historical purpose. The transition from communism to capitalism was never going to be smooth. The totalitarian order established by [the first head of the Soviet state, Vladimir] Lenin and [Soviet dictator Joseph] Stalin was so formidable and so deeply rooted in the Soviet psyche that it could not be demolished head-on. To remain in power and continue his reforms, Gorbachev had to proceed by stealth. This master of Kremlin intrigue bobbed and weaved among the rival factions, hiding his true intentions beneath a fog of Communist rhetoric. Duplicity and [mystification] were his required talents; political survival was the supreme imperative. Had he been clearer about his goals, it is likely that his Politburo colleagues would have attempted to get rid of him much earlier. By the time they finally understood what was happening, it was too late. The party had been destroyed from within.

The Soviet Communist Party was prepared to fight to remain in power as long as this was a serious option. The repressive power of the totalitarian state meant that domestic rebellions could be ruthlessly crushed. From the moment such a state possessed nuclear weapons, it became invulnerable to foreign invasion. The only way out, therefore, was death by economic exhaustion.

The Fatal Blow

The irony is that the last general secretary had to fail in order to succeed in the larger historical mission of vanquishing communism. Gorbachev came to power promising to reverse several decades of Soviet economic decline and revitalize the Marxist-Leninist [Communist] idea. Had he succeeded, the system would have received a new or at least a temporary lease on life. There would have been less pressure for significant political reform. The deepening economic crisis made the transition to democracy possible but also fraught with danger because it left many people yearning for the security of the authoritarian past.

In the long run the collapse of Soviet communism was inevitable, for the simple reason that it was too top-heavy a structure to bear its own weight. But there was nothing inevitable about the timing of the collapse or the manner in which it occurred. History will record that it was Gorbachev who set in motion the chain of events that led to the disintegration of the world's first socialist state. Through a strange amalgam [mixture] of genius and incompetence, idealism and egotism, naiveté and cunning, the onetime peasant boy from Privolnoye dealt a fatal blow to the most durable dictatorship humankind has ever known.

By seeking to reinvigorate the Communist system, Gorbachev succeeded in destroying it.

The Coup of 1991 Was a Failure

The Economist

In the following viewpoint, the Moscow correspondent for a British periodical attributes the failure of the 1991 attempt to overthrow the government of Mikhail Gorbachev to a lack of ruthlessness and planning by the junta responsible for the coup. The only person of consequence they arrested was Mikhail Gorbachev. They did not arrest Russian president Boris Yeltsin, who publicly denounced the coup, and their failure to act decisively early on gave Yeltsin supporters a chance to come together and press for resistance. They did not shut down the media; did nothing to secure Leningrad, the second largest Soviet city; and took no action to put a stop to the surge in active resistance in Moscow and Leningrad. Junta leaders rapidly lost control of one part of the country after another because they chose not to assert their authority and act with more military precision and callousness.

SOURCE. "Anatomy of a Botched Coup," *The Economist*, August 24, 1991, pp. 17–19. Copyright © 1991 by The Economist. Republished with permission of *The Economist*, conveyed through Copyright Clearance Center, Inc.

Helicopters beat the air over Moscow for days before. But the eve of the coup was Soviet Air Force Day, so no one thought twice about them. The announcement on the morning of Monday August 19th that [Soviet President] Mikhail Gorbachev, holidaying in the Crimea, was "ill" and that his duties had been taken over by his vice-president came out of a blue sky.

Yet the coup not only could have been predicted, it was—by Mr Gorbachev's former adviser, Alexander Yakovlev, who resigned from the Communist Party on August 16th, giving warning that the party was preparing a "Stalinist coup".

An Unconstitutional Coup

He was wrong about the party. The state of emergency was imposed by a junta consisting of the prime minister, the heads of the three security services (defence ministry, KGB [Committee for State Security], interior ministry) and representatives of the "military-industrial complex", the vast chunk of the economy controlled by the armed forces. The usurping vice-president, Gennadi Yanaev, tried to portray it as ordinary constitutional procedure following the illness of the president. But the semblance of constitutionality was a fiction.

The timing made clear the purpose of the coup. That Monday, Mr Gorbachev was due back in Moscow, intending to sign a new union treaty the next day. The treaty would

> Though the day of the coup must have been decided some time in advance, it was poorly prepared and conspicuously lacking in military precision.

have delegated nearly all significant central-government powers to the republics, which were to be recognised as "sovereigns states". The junta's first decree was that the constitution of the Soviet Union took precedence over republican ones, and that decisions of the

ПАТРИОТ

ЕЖЕНЕДЕЛЬНАЯ ГАЗЕТА НАРОДНО-ПАТРИОТИЧЕСКИХ СИЛ РОССИИ

МЫ — НАСТОЯЩИЕ!

A decade after their failed 1991 coup, the organizers publicly regretted their reluctance to use force against the general population. (**AP Images.**)

emergency committee had to be obeyed by republican governments.

A Lack of Ruthlessness and Planning

Yet, though the day of the coup must have been decided some time in advance, it was poorly prepared and conspicuously lacking in military precision. Tanks did not appear in the streets of Moscow until nearly midday, six hours after the announcement of Mr Gorbachev's "illness". And when units of the Taman motorised rifle division and the Katemirov airborne division did roll into the city, it was in an uncoordinated jam, with tanks queuing up [lining up] two and three abreast for miles along Moscow's outer ring road.

The lack of ruthlessness and planning became more and more apparent as the hours passed. The only person of significance arrested was Mr Gorbachev himself. Boris Yeltsin, Russia's president, was left free to lead the opposition. He went to his parliament building, known as the White House, where he denounced the coup and called for a general strike. The failure to arrest Mr Yeltsin reveals the committee's blurriness of purpose: until he uttered his defiance, Mr Yeltsin had broken none of the committee's decrees; when he did, it was too late to arrest him. . . .

Telephone lines remained open and miners' leaders inside the Russian parliament began to organise strikes by telephone.

Western press and television operated freely. The junta even lost control of its own media. No soldiers arrived to censor the opposition press, even though the junta had said that all but eight newspapers were being closed down. The next day several liberal newspapers banded together to bring out a special joint edition. On the day of the coup itself Soviet television viewers were regaled with the sight of Mr Yanaev being asked what he thought of Mr Yeltsin's call for a national strike—which broadcast the strike call over the country.

Those first few hours of dithering were decisive, because they gave Mr Yeltsin's supporters a chance to rally. In the early hours of the coup it seemed that even the tanks had failed to rouse the Russians out of their famous passivity. Inside the Russian parliament people were playing computer games. The massed demonstrations that filled the centre of Moscow earlier in the year to support Mr Yeltsin failed to materialise. No rattle of gunfire sounded in the streets. . . .

Two Factors that Turned the Tide

Yet, from Monday afternoon onwards, every hour that went by saw the committee losing control of one part of the country after another. First the strike began to take hold as miners in half the pits in Russia's main mining areas walked out. Within a day of the coup the garrison commanders of 11 Russian cities opted to support Mr Yeltsin. Then the republics, too, began to line

> The failure to storm the parliament was a test that the junta failed.

up behind him. Even part of the Communist Party entered the fray against the coup when its deputy leader, Vladimir Ivashko, demanded to see Mr Gorbachev.

By midday on Tuesday, the second day of the coup, it still seemed possible that its leaders, given enough ruthlessness, could assert their authority. At this point, with events hanging in the balance, two things tipped the advantage to Mr Yeltsin.

The first was the appearance of serious dissatisfaction in the upper levels of the armed forces. . . .

Imposing a coup in a country as large as the Soviet Union means relying on local commanders. Their willingness to obey orders varied. In the Baltic states General Fedor Kuzmin, accustomed to violence after the events in Lithuania in January, sent his troops to all three capitals. But in Georgia the independence-seeking president persuaded the local commander not to deploy his troops by disbanding Georgia's own national guard. Leningrad's mayor . . . persuaded the military commander there . . . to allow mass demonstrations in the centre of the city by promising not to call for a strike (which went ahead anyway at several plants). The junta's inability to secure the country's second [largest] city was extraordinary evidence of its failure of will.

Significantly, during the whole 60-hour fiasco nothing was heard from the chief of staff, General Mikhail Moiseev (who was appointed acting defence minister after the coup failed). The likely explanation is that he was unwilling to throw the full weight of the armed forces behind the putsch [sudden attempt to overthrow the government].

But this alone was not enough to explain its collapse. The second thing that decided the issue was the surge in active resistance in Moscow and Leningrad. This meant that the coup could succeed only through the most ruthless oppression. And that was something the coup leaders were unwilling, or unable, to order. . . .

A Fatal Loss of Nerve

General [Vladimir] Kryuchkov himself, according to a Russian KGB officer, decided not to storm the parliament. . . .

The failure to storm the parliament was a test that the junta failed. Unwilling to fill the streets with blood, yet unable to control the country in any other way, the conspirators turned against each other. A baffling series of rumours began, with one member after another reported to have left the group. First the prime minister was said to be ill and to have been replaced by his deputy (this was true). The defence minister and the KGB chief were said to have stepped down (this was not true). But even the rumours were revealing, because they pointed—correctly—to the junta's loss of nerve. . . .

This was not a carefully prepared counter-revolution, using full military force. It was a botched continuation of an abortive constitutional coup d'état that had taken place a month earlier. On June 17th the prime minister asked parliament to reduce Mr Gorbachev's powers, and was supported by the men who made up this week's junta. Parliament rejected the demand and President Gorbachev, flanked by the defence, KGB and police chiefs, laughingly observed that "the coup is over". At last, it really is.

The Vote of the Soviet People Could Not Preserve the Union

James Platt, Translator

In a March 1991 referendum a majority of Soviet citizens voted to preserve the Soviet Union. Their vote was not enough to stop the breakup of the Soviet Union into fifteen independent states. The eight Russian politicians, scholars, and political analysts who express their opinions in the following viewpoint from the Russian newspaper *Pravda* do not agree entirely on why the referendum vote made no difference and who was to blame for the breakup. Several contend that the people had no intention of bringing about the collapse of the state and that responsibility for the breakup lies with the elites, some of whom put their personal interests first. The August 1991 coup played a role as well. If it had not taken place, the Union might have been preserved in one form or another. The will and decisiveness needed to defend the constitution was lacking.

On the same spring day of 17th March 1991 a majority of Soviet citizens (76 per cent) voted in a referendum to preserve the USSR. This declaration of the people's will was consigned to history, as in reality everything turned out exactly the opposite: several months later the Union fell apart and instead of one state, 15 new ones were formed. Moreover, the Russian Federation was the first to declare its sovereignty. Why did things happen in this way? Who is to blame? What would have happened if the referendum had worked in practice, and not just remained on paper? Here are the views of some famous politicians, scholars and political analysts on these questions.

The Elites Bear the Blame

Yuriy Ryzhov, President of the International University of Engineering: The elites were already prepared for the fact that they would come out from under Moscow's control. But the people were for maintaining the Union and I think that today they would have voted in just the same way. The elites of the national republics understood that the Union could not be maintained in the same form as it existed at that time, but then it would gradually be transformed without any major cataclysms. The August Putsch [1991 coup] created an explosive situation, it terrified the national elites, and all the republics immediately went their own separate ways.

Sergey Karaganov, Deputy Director of the European Institute RAN: Why did the referendum not work? Because by that time the Soviet elite had dissolved, it had lost its link with its motherland. This was a result of the failure of the Communist experiment. The national elites [had] been torn apart in all directions. The fun-

> The referendum should have been followed up with political actions: all the organs of power should have been dissolved and new ones should have been elected.

damental role in the collapse of the USSR was played by the vote in the Supreme Council of the RSFSR [Russian Soviet Federative Socialist Republic] in favour of Russia's independence. Let me remind you that all different factions voted in favour, from the Communists to those on the right. As it turns out, the Soviet Union could only have been maintained through violent means, but no one resolved to carry out this option.

The Putsch Was Responsible

Vladimir Lukin, Human Rights Commissioner in Russia: The referendum should have been followed up with political actions: all the organs of power should have been dissolved and new ones should have been elected. This was not done, no measures were taken as a result of the referendum. That is why it did not work.

Aleksey Podberezkin, Senior Academic Specialist for the Institute of Civil Society: A section of the Soviet elite, including members of the party, put their personal interests first. Everyone wanted to have their own Central Banks, embassies, did not want to pay taxes into the state coffers—like in Ukraine, Kazakhstan. . . . Yes, Russia voted for sovereignty, but it did not want the Union to collapse (I know, as I was an advisor to [Russian President Boris] Yeltsin at the time). Following the putsch [coup] the national elites made de facto declarations of independence. It all went down that route because there was not enough will or decisiveness at the centre to defend the Constitution—for example by means of force. President Gorbachev could not and did not want to do that. Now he explains that it was because he did [not] want any blood to be spilt.

> People are just being sly when they say that everyone voted for the USSR: everyone had their own interpretation of what the preservation of the Union actually meant.

The Past Is Past

The further the events of fifteen years ago [1991]—that is, the disintegration of the Soviet Union and the creation of the loose association called the Commonwealth of Independent States [CIS] in its place—retreat into history, the less definite the population's assessments of these events become, their concept of the future of the post-Soviet space, and the greater the differences of the views of the inhabitants of the former Soviet republics regarding these things. . . .

Throughout these fifteen years, positive and negative assessments of the disintegration of the Soviet Union have fluctuated in accordance with the events of domestic and international life. Nonetheless, one clear tendency can be discerned: the older generations have more regrets than the younger ones about the country's disintegration. In addition, fewer and fewer young people are interested in the past at all, including the Soviet past, and for many of them the disintegration of the Soviet Union is history as ancient as the Revolution of 1917. Accordingly, almost one-fifth of Russians—mostly those younger than twenty-five—find it difficult to give any assessment of the liquidation of the Soviet Union. And 10 percent of the respondents in Russia do not even know that the Soviet Union fell apart fifteen years ago and that the CIS was formed. Such people total 7 percent in Belarus and 19 percent in Ukraine.

SOURCE: *N.P. Popov, "Nostalgia for Greatness—Russia in the Post-Soviet Space,"* Sociological Research *47, no. 5 (September–October 2008), pp. 36–51.*

Deputy of the State Duma Vladimir Ryzhkov: The main reason for the collapse of the union is the putsch that occurred in August [1991]. If [USSR Vice President

Genadii] Yanaev, [Vladimir] Kryuchkov [KGB chief] and his company had not set up the State Emergency Committee, then in some form the Union would have been preserved. Everyone apart from the Baltic states [Estonia, Latvia, Lithuania] was prepared to support it. But one after another the republics began to declare their sovereignty. It is the putschists who bear the main responsibility for the collapse of the USSR, not Gorbachev.

The Referendum Was a Stimulus

Andranik Migranyan, Vice-President of the "Reform" Fund and Member of the Public Chamber of the Russian Federation: The referendum on preserving the Union was carried out in the period when the Federal centre and Gorbachev had entirely lost control over the coun-

Russian Human Rights Commissioner Vladimir Lukin (left), pictured here with Russian president Dmitry Medvedev, cited a lack of political action by the electorate after the referendum on the USSR's continued existence. (**AP Images.**)

try. People are just being sly when they say that everyone voted for the USSR: everyone had their own interpretation of what the preservation of the Union actually meant. Incidentally, it was because through this very referendum that Yeltsin gained the opportunity to run for the post of president and bring about the disintegration of the country. This was a result of Gorbachev's policy which had led to a total loss of control over the processes which were unfolding in the country. And after the referendum all the republics interpreted those questions which they themselves had included in it. The federal centre did not act because by that time it was already an impotent force. Even if 100 per cent had voted to preserve the Union, then because of those questions which had been included in the republics, the Union was doomed. The referendum became a stimulus for the collapse of the USSR.

Irina Khamakada, Politician: If the results of the referendum 15 years ago had been implemented, then Gorbachev would have remained president, and the Russian Den Syaponin, not Yeltsin, would have come to power in Russia.

Active Minorities and Political Elites Decided

Konstantin Zatulin, State Duma Deputy, Director of the Institute for CIS Countries: The question which was asked in the referendum was by that time decided not by the peoples, but by elites. The Soviet elite was in absolutely total disorder. Many "bonzes" were not interested in preserving the Union. In this the Russian elite, which had begun to form on the back of the negation of the Soviet centre's authority, set the example. And the total loss of guidelines, the lack of understanding of the aims behind perestroika [restructuring] and failure of the reforms played their role. With all due respect to Mikhail

Sergeevich [Gorbachev] it is now clear that Gorbachev did not entirely know what his policy was aiming towards and did not imagine the costs and risks which lay on this path. He managed to defeat the old brigade in the Politburo, but awoke forces which he was incapable of opposing, in fact he did not even suspect that they existed, and in the end he lost.

The referendum is a historical fact, a document which takes the blame off the main mass of the population of the Soviet Union. They had absolutely no intention of bringing about the collapse of the state. The striving for independence in various parts of the USSR were extremely localized, it was linked to local circumstances, say in the Baltic states, in Georgia. But this did not reflect the mood of the people in Ukraine, Belorussia [now Belarus], Kazakhstan, that is to say the main areas which formed the system of the former Soviet Union. The main significance of this referendum is that people came out in support of the preservation of the USSR. But as in most cases in the political process it is not the abstract people who make decisions, however many of them there may be, but the active minorities and political elites, the elites were victorious. They made the most of a succession of failures of the central authority and in the end brought about the end of this central authority and the entire state.

Today [2006] the following ideas are mentioned: if not to go as far as restoring the Soviet Union, then perhaps we should at least create a Unified state of Russia and Belorussia, and carry out a referendum on the unification. But [what] will be the point of such a referendum, if the elites have not agreed? When there is this agreement, then it will be possible to carry out referenda.

Russia's Sovereignty Destroyed the Soviet Union

Seweryn Bialer

In this viewpoint, written in 1990, Sovietologist Seweryn Bialer maintains that the Russian parliament's declaration of sovereignty destroyed the Soviet Union. While the call for independence by other republics was important, it did not have the impact of Russia's actions. Russia ruled the Soviet Union and ran the Soviet Communist Party. When the Soviet Union lost Russia, it lost its legitimacy and its only power base. Whether Soviet president Mikhail Gorbachev chose to acknowledge it or not, the Soviet Union no longer was governable, not in its whole nor in its parts. Seweryn Bialer is professor of political science at Columbia University and director of Columbia's Research Institute on International Change. An expert on the Communist parties of the Soviet Union and Poland, he has written numerous articles and books on Soviet government and policy.

SOURCE. Seweryn Bialer, "Russia vs. the Soviet Union: by Declaring Its Independence from the Kremlin, the Russian Heartland Has Destroyed the U.S.S.R.," *U.S. News & World Report*, November 5, 1990. Copyright © 1990 U.S. News & World Report, L.P. All rights reserved. Reprinted with permission.

The Soviet Union, which claims sovereignty over one sixth of the globe and 290 million people, has virtually disintegrated. The dissolution of the political, economic and cultural ties between the center and the periphery, among the 15 republics and even within the Russian heartland itself, has achieved a momentum of its own that [Soviet president] Mikhail Gorbachev cannot stop and is not willing, or does not know how, to accommodate.

The Quest for Sovereignty

All 14 non-Russian republics have declared their sovereignty and proclaimed the supremacy of their own authority over that of the Soviet government in Moscow, but Gorbachev is still clinging to the belief that power flows from the center to the periphery. He wants to reform the Union by delegating specific rights and greater autonomy to the republics, but the republics are insisting that they will delegate powers and rights to Gorbachev and his central government, if there is to be one. Gorbachev's political relevance and ultimately his survival now depend on what the republics will grant him. Unless, of course, he is willing and able to use massive violence.

With every passing week, the claims of sovereignty are becoming more radical and all-embracing. . . .

The quest for sovereignty is no longer confined to the democratic and nationalist forces. The centrist and even conservative leaderships that remain dominant in many republics and are still the largest force in the Ukraine and Byelorussia [now Belarus] have also embraced the principle. . . .

Trouble in the Heartland

The most important declaration of soverignty, however, has taken place not on the non-Russian periphery but in Russia itself, in the very heart of the Soviet Union. The

Russian parliament's declaration of sovereignty is a revolutionary watershed. It has, in fact, destroyed the Soviet Union.

> **Russia was the Soviet Union.**

Russia was the Soviet Union. The Russian Republic was the first among the 15, and Russian authority and Soviet rule were synonymous. The Russians ruled the Soviet Union, while local non-Russian Communist elites ran the day-to-day affairs of their own regions. Each republic had its own Communist party; the Russians did not need a separate party because they ran the entire Communist Party of the Soviet Union.

Now there are two Moscows: Moscow of the Kremlin, the capital of the Soviet Union, where foreign dignitaries pay their respects to President Gorbachev, and Moscow the capital of the Russian Republic, housed in a white building [where the] Kremlin represents the past; its contract with the people has been terminated, or at least suspended. The capital of Russia represents the Russian people, but nobody else. The Moscow of the Kremlin still has all the accouterments and instruments of power, and it is still feared. But when it lost the homeland of the Russians, it lost both its legitimacy and its only power base.

Russia's declaration of sovereignty and its growing independence are sometimes attributed primarily to the ambitions of the leader of Russia, Boris Yeltsin, Gorbachev's most prominent opponent. But the roots and the meaning of the Russian position go much deeper. . . .

The demise of Russian domestic imperialism and the disintegration of the Soviet Union would be relatively clean-cut were it not for another legacy of the imperial past reinforced by the 70 years of totalitarian Communism—the ethnic diversity of the republics. When Russia declared its independence from the Soviet

Boris Yeltsin (left) was the most prominent national leader hostile to Soviet rule. (Alain-Pierre Hovasse/AFP/Getty Images.)

Union, it called into question its own authority over significant parts of its own territory and population.

Some 25 million non-Russians are concentrated in separate administrative units called autonomous republics or regions within the Russian Republic. Motivated by the same emotions, passions and self-interests that have led the Soviet republics on their separatist paths, many of these units are in the process of declaring their sovereignty within Russia. . . .

An Ungovernable Union

Even where national and ethnic aspirations are not at issue, executive power is collapsing at every level. The Soviet Union has become ungovernable, either as a whole or in parts. Rural areas want independence from urban centers, boroughs from cities, towns from regions, regions from republics, areas of extractive industries (oil, coal, gold, etc.) from everybody else. Executive power, whether it is in the hands of conservatives or democratic reformers, remains toothless and inchoate.

Unless this centrifugal trend is reversed, the fragmentation of the society, polity and economy will accelerate, with violence just around the corner. Not even the most radical market or democratic reforms will have a chance.

> Can a reformed Soviet Union, with a strong central authority, reemerge?

Is confederation next? Can a reformed Soviet Union, with a strong central authority, reemerge? Probably not. The point of no return has been reached, even if Gorbachev's government stops simply reacting to events and begins trying to take command of the situation. At some point, a confederation of the national republics may emerge, but it is unlikely to include all 15 of the Soviet Union's present republics.

Yeltsin, the leader of the most powerful republic, and the most important figures around him now want an agreement with other republics to create some form of a federal authority. If the present impasse with the Gorbachev government persists, however, the republics will be forced to find their own ways to integrate and reform their economies. If that continues, the new ties among them will be formed in direct negotiations, not through Gorbachev's mediation.

The only other force available to hold together either parts of the union or a new confederation with a strong central government is the military, the only real instrument of mass power still in Gorbachev's hands. Force and intimidation can be effective against the power of ideas and of loosely organized social and political groups. But it is unclear whether the military can act and succeed, and whether it will act on its own. The authority of the Army and the KGB has declined significantly. The Army leadership has been unable to keep the national and political passions out of the armed forces, not only among draftees but also among the professional officer corps. The mass mobilization of national fervor outside Russia, the rejection of the old order and the organization of large segments of workers especially those in the oil and coal industries) inside Russia and the Ukraine, and the deterioration of the Army itself all have reached a level where the Army would be foolish to attempt a massive domestic crackdown. . . .

Gorbachev's Options

To save what he [Gorbachev] believes can and must be saved, the Soviet leader is moving closer and closer to enlarging emergency presidential rule. If, as seems likely, decrees and orders continue to be ineffective, Gorbachev may show no more determination than he has so far, and let the disintegration continue apace. But he may consider this his last chance to restore a modicum of economic and social order. If so, his most likely option will be to suspend the Moscow and Leningrad soviets, and even the Russian parliament, and to put himself in charge.

But if these and other institutions refuse to comply with his orders, Gorbachev cannot continue without martial law. He may expect that people, tired of shortages, crime and chaos, will acquiesce when presented with the promise of order.

Nothing in these scenarios is inevitable. What is certain, however, is that the choices are becoming starker and the confrontations deeper. The democratic forces in Moscow are growing apprehensive, but whether central Soviet authority will end with a whimper or try to save itself with a bang remains to be seen.

The Soviet Union Was Abolished for Political and Personal Gain

Stephen Cohen

In the following viewpoint, academic and author Stephen Cohen contends that Russian leader Boris Yeltsin, with the support of the Soviet elite, put an end to the Soviet Union. The way in which Yeltsin accomplished this was "neither legitimate nor democratic." Most Soviets did not want the Soviet Union to come to an end. Yeltsin, they claimed, overthrew the Soviet state for political gain. His goal was to get rid of Soviet president Mikhail Gorbachev. The Russian bureaucratic elites supported the overthrow for personal gain. They wanted Soviet property and were more interested in privatizing the state's vast wealth than in defending it. They wanted a political system along the lines of a "managed democracy," not Gorbachev's system of parliamentary electoral democracy. Stephen Cohen is professor

SOURCE. Stephen Cohen, "The breakup of the Soviet Union ended Russia's march to democracy: Putin's Russia can only be understood in the light of the national collapse triggered by the dissolution of the USSR," *The Guardian*, December 13, 2006, p. 25. Copyright © 2006 Guardian Newspapers Limited. Reproduced by permission of Guardian News Service, LTD.

of Russian and Slavic studies at New York University and author of several books, including *Failed Crusade: America and the Tragedy of Post-Communist Russia.*

The most consequential event of the second half of the 20th century took place 15 years ago at a secluded hunting lodge in the Belovezh Forest near Minsk. On December 8 1991, heads of three of the Soviet Union's 15 republics, led by Russia's Boris Yeltsin, met there to sign documents abolishing that 74-year-old state.

The Western View

For most western commentators the Soviet breakup was an unambiguously positive turning point in Russian and world history. As it quickly became the defining moment in a new American triumphalist narrative, the hope that Mikhail Gorbachev's pro-Soviet democratic and market reforms of 1985–91 would succeed was forgotten. Soviet history was now presented as "Russia's seven decades as a rigid and ruthless police state". American academics reacted similarly, most reverting to pre-Gorbachev axioms that the system had always been unreformable and doomed. The opposing view that there had been other possibilities in Soviet history, "roads not taken", was dismissed as a "dubious", if not disloyal, notion. Gorbachev's reforms, despite having so remarkably dismantled the Communist party dictatorship, had been "a chimera" [fantasy], and the Soviet Union therefore died from a "lack of alternatives".

Most specialists no longer asked, even in the light of the human tragedies that followed in the 1990s, if a reforming Soviet Union might have been the best hope for the post-

> *A large majority of Russians . . . regret the end of the Soviet Union, not because they pine for 'communism' but because they lost a secure way of life.*

communist future of Russia. Nor have mainstream commentators asked if its survival would have been better for world affairs. On the contrary, they concluded that everything Soviet had to be discarded by "the razing of the entire edifice of political and economic relations". Such certitudes are now, of course, the only politically correct ones in US (and most European) policy, media and academic circles.

The Russian View

A large majority of Russians, on the other hand, as they have regularly made clear in opinion surveys, regret the end of the Soviet Union, not because they pine for "communism" but because they lost a secure way of life. They do not share the nearly unanimous western view that the Soviet Union's "collapse" was "inevitable" because of inherent fatal defects. They believe instead, and for good reason, that three "subjective" factors broke it up: the way Gorbachev carried out his political and economic reforms; a power struggle in which Yeltsin overthrew the Soviet state in order to get rid of its president, Gorbachev; and

> Yeltsin abolished the Soviet Union with the backing of the nomenklatura elites—pursuing the 'smell of property like a beast after prey.'

property-seizing Soviet bureaucratic elites, the nomenklatura, who were more interested in "privatising" the state's enormous wealth in 1991 than in defending it. Most Russians, including even the imprisoned oligarch Mikhail Khodorkovsky, therefore still see December 1991 as a "tragedy".

In addition, a growing number of Russian intellectuals have come to believe that something essential was lost—a historic opportunity to democratise and modernise Russia by methods more gradualist, consensual and less traumatic, and thus more fruitful and less costly, than those adopted after 1991.

Photo on previous page: Putting his own ambitions before concern for the state, Boris Yeltsin (center) wrested power from Mikhail Gorbachev in 1991. (**AP Images.**)

One common post-Soviet myth, promoted by Yeltsin's supporters, is that the dissolution was "peaceful". In reality, ethnic civil wars erupted in central Asia and Transcaucasia, killing hundreds of thousands and brutally displacing even more, a process still under way.

Yeltsin, Parliament, and the Economy

It is hard to imagine a political act more extreme than abolishing what was still, for all its crises, a nuclear superpower state of 286 million citizens. And yet Yeltsin did it, as even his sympathisers acknowledged, in a way that was "neither legitimate nor democratic".

Having ended the Soviet state in a way that lacked legal or popular legitimacy—in a referendum nine months before, 76% had voted to preserve the union—the Yeltsin ruling group soon became fearful of real democracy. And indeed Yeltsin's armed overthrow of the Russian parliament soon followed.

The economic dimensions of Belovezh were no less portentous. Dissolving the union without any preparatory stages shattered a highly integrated economy and was a major cause of the collapse of production across the former Soviet territories, which fell by almost half in the 1990s. That in turn contributed to mass poverty and its attendant social pathologies, which are still, in the words of a respected Moscow economist, the "main fact" of Russian life today.

Property and Politics

And, as a one-time Yeltsin supporter wrote later, "almost everything that happened in Russia after 1991 was determined to a significant extent by the divvying-up of the property of the former USSR". Soviet elites took much of the state's enormous wealth with no regard for fair procedures or public opinion. To enrich themselves, they wanted the most valuable state property distributed from above, without the participation of legislatures. They achieved that, first by themselves, through "spontaneous nomenklatura privatisation", and after 1991, through Kremlin decrees issued by Yeltsin.

Fearful for their dubiously acquired assets and even for their lives, the new property holders were as determined as Yeltsin to limit or reverse the parliamentary electoral democracy initiated by Gorbachev. In its place they strove to create a political system devoted to and corrupted by their wealth, at best a "managed" democracy. . . .

So why did so many western commentators hail the breakup of the Soviet Union as a "breakthrough" to democracy? Their reaction was based mainly on anti-communist ideology and hopeful myths.

Yeltsin abolished the Soviet Union with the backing of the nomenklatura elites—pursuing the "smell of property like a beast after prey", as Yeltsin's chief minister put it—and an avowedly pro-democracy wing of the intelligentsia. Traditional enemies in the pre-Gorbachev Soviet system, they colluded in 1991 largely because the intelligentsia's radical market ideas seemed to justify nomenklatura privatisation.

But the most influential pro-Yeltsin intellectuals were neither coincidental fellow travellers nor real democrats. Since the late 1980s they had insisted that free-market economics and large-scale private property would have to be imposed on Russian society by an "iron hand" regime using "anti-democratic measures". Like the property-seeking elites, they saw Russia's newly elected legislatures as an obstacle. Admirers of Chile's Augusto Pinochet, they said of Yeltsin: "Let him be a dictator!" Not surprisingly, they cheered (along with the US government and mainstream media) when he used tanks to destroy Russia's popularly elected parliament in 1993.

Political and economic alternatives still existed in Russia after 1991, and none of the factors contributing to the end of the Soviet Union were inexorable. But even if democratic and market aspirations were among them, so were cravings for power, political coups, elite avarice, extremist ideas and widespread perceptions of illegitimacy and betrayal. It should have been clear which would prevail.

The Outside World Contributed to the Soviet Collapse

Robert Strayer

In the following viewpoint, Robert Strayer contends in 1998 that external pressures—pressures stemming from the outside world—contributed to the collapse of the Soviet Union. Although these pressures did not actually cause the collapse, they played a part in internal processes that undermined the Soviet system. American foreign policy, a drop in world oil prices, and the growing penetration of Western popular culture all had an impact. Other foreign involvement, such as the war in Afghanistan, was another contributing factor. The war in particular damaged the image of the Soviet Union both internationally and internally. Yet another development in the outside world that had a deep impact on the Soviet Union itself was the ending of communism in Eastern Europe. Robert Strayer is professor of world history and has written several books and articles on world history,

---

SOURCE. Robert Strayer, *Why Did the Soviet Union Collapse?: Understanding Historical Change.* Armonk, NY: M.E. Sharpe, 1998. Copyright © 1998 by M.E. Sharpe, Inc. All rights reserved. Reproduced by permission.

including *Why Did the Soviet Union Collapse?: Understanding Historical Change.*

Most analysis of the Soviet collapse focuses on matters internal to the country and argues that its demise was self-induced. But was the end of the Soviet Union conditioned by external pressures as well? Did the outside world significantly contribute to the Soviet collapse? One answer to this question, argued passionately by American Cold War "hawks" [supporters of the war] held that newly aggressive Reagan administration policies in the early 1980s won the Cold War for the West and in the process drove a weakening Soviet Union to ruin. According to one account, the Reagan team, spearheaded by CIA [Central Intelligence Agency] director William Casey, formulated an explicit "secret strategy" to exacerbate Soviet weaknesses and undermine Soviet power: a costly high-tech military buildup, intended to bankrupt the Soviet Union; economic warfare by opposing Soviet oil and gas sales to Western Europe and by lowering, in cooperation with Saudia Arabia, the world price of oil, thus denying the USSR badly needed foreign currency from one of its major exports; financial assistance to Solidarity [non-communist trade union] in Poland and military assistance, including Stinger antiaircraft missiles, to the Afghan resistance movement; and a challenge to the USSR's moral legitimacy by declaring it an "evil empire." In this view, the country did not simply self-destruct; it was defeated.

The Debate on American Foreign Policy and the Soviet Collapse

How should we evaluate such an argument? On the one hand, a number of Soviet-era leaders have themselves stated that American policies "accelerated" the country's decline and were a "catalyst" for its collapse.

And few observers would doubt that Soviet military spending, running at some 15–25 percent of a GNP [gross national product] roughly half the size of the American economy, contributed to its economic stagnation. Furthermore, [Soviet leader Mikhail] Gorbachev made no secret of his desire for a less hostile international

> "The debate about the Soviet collapse remains thoroughly entangled with the long controversy over American foreign policy during the Cold War."

environment generally and for sharp limits on the American SDI [Strategic Defense Initiative] project in particular. Only such conditions, he argued, would allow him to reshape the budgetary priorities of the USSR and promote real reform. And a drop in world oil prices in the mid-1980s surely damaged Gorbachev's economic reforms by sharply reducing the country's hard currency earnings.

But critics of hard-line American policies, sometimes dubbed Cold War "doves," [those opposed to the war] have sharply contested such a self-congratulatory analysis. Those policies, they note, had produced only Soviet intransigence [resistance] before Gorbachev's arrival on the political scene. Thus, the credit for ending the Cold War should go to Gorbachev rather than Reagan. Furthermore, they argue that American refusal to restrict its SDI project and the rush toward German reunification strengthened conservative forces in the Soviet Union and undermined Gorbachev's position. Such policies, coupled with the growing penetration of western culture, gave credence to conservative arguments that Gorbachev had "sold out," compromised the country's independence, and opened it to western decadence. A more accommodating policy might have helped both Gorbachev and a democratizing Soviet Union to survive and thus avoided the ethnic conflicts and threats of nuclear proliferation that accompanied its collapse. And the doves simply disagree about the relative importance of American policies in explaining the Soviet collapse. At most, those policies represented an added strain on the Soviet economy, but the country's internal weaknesses were far more important. Thus the debate about the Soviet collapse remains thoroughly entangled with the long controversy over American foreign policy during the Cold War.

The Impact of Societal and Cultural Comparison

Still another point of view holds that the West conditioned the Soviet collapse less through direct pressures from governments than by simply providing an alternative and more successful model of modern society. Both political leaders and educated citizens in the USSR increasingly saw their country's technological development, its standard of living, and its international standing in the mirror of superior western achievements. That highly unflattering comparison both eroded the legitimacy of the Soviet system in their eyes and prompted Gorbachev's vigorous efforts to rectify the situation. He called repeatedly for the Soviet economy to match "world standards," which were in fact western standards. Those who retained a commitment to socialism now referred to Swedish or Austrian models as they abandoned Leninism. Comparisons operated as well in cultural matters. Particularly for younger people, the attractions of western popular culture—TV, movies, rock and roll, jeans, and T-shirts—and its permissive lifestyle "seduced the communist world far more effectively than ideological sermons by anticommunist activists."

All of these comparisons, of course, derived from the greater knowledge of the West made possible by

> In 1950 only 2 percent of Soviet citizens had shortwave radios, but by 1980 at least half of the population could tune into these broadcasts.

increased travel, tourism, and exchanges, as well as by information obtained from European and American radio services such as the BBC, Voice of America, and Radio Free Europe. In 1950 only 2 percent of Soviet citizens had shortwave radios, but by 1980 at least half of the population could tune into these broadcasts. Soviet isolation was breaking down.

War in Afghanistan and Events in China

Beyond the West, other foreign involvement may have contributed to the Soviet collapse as well. One was the war in Afghanistan. Originating in 1979 as an effort to stabilize a recently imposed pro-Soviet regime, that war became the USSR's Vietnam, a "bleeding wound" in Gorbachev's words, until the Soviet withdrawal in 1988–89. It shredded the Soviet Union's propaganda image as a "peace-loving" country and drew bitter criticism not only from the West but also from the Third World and even from many other communist parties. That criticism contributed to the international isolation of the Soviet Union that Gorbachev set out to overcome. Even more important, failure to overwhelm the Afghan resistance devastated the proud image of the Soviet military. Mounting casualties, numbering some twenty thousand to fifty thousand killed, sowed doubts about the Soviet regime in the minds of many people, despite the absence of an overt antiwar movement. Widespread drug abuse and the physical and psychological traumas suffered by many Soviet veterans also brought the costs of that conflict home.

Events in the communist world and elsewhere as well echoed in the Soviet Union during its final decade. China's vigorous reforms predated Gorbachev's efforts by six years and far surpassed Soviet policies in their economic success. China in fact became a model that Gorbachev's critics used to good effect. Free-market advocates pointed to China's decollectivization of agri-

Tens of thousands of Soviet soldiers were killed in the Afghanistan war, devistating the army's image of invicibility. (Danil Semyonov/ AFP/Getty Images.)

culture, while conservatives focused attention on China's ability to retain party control of the reform process. The Chile of General Augusto Pinochet, who combined free-market policies with a highly authoritarian political system, also surfaced in discussions about alternatives to Gorbachev's approach.

Three Undermining International Processes

But outside of the western world and Afghanistan, the most consequential international developments occurred in Eastern Europe, where communist regimes everywhere dissolved during 1989. Soviet policies under Gorbachev had both stimulated and permitted that disintegration, but once it was accomplished, the collapse of communism there had a deep impact on the Soviet Union itself. It encouraged and emboldened nationalists in the "inner empire." Why could Lithuanians and Georgians not achieve what Poland and Czechoslovakia had? And it infuriated conservatives who saw treachery and betrayal in the loss of the "outer empire."

Thus, the international environment in which the Soviet Union operated in the 1980s, while not itself decisive in causing the country's collapse, contributed to three internal processes that fundamentally undermined the Soviet system: the declining legitimacy of the communist regime in the eyes of its own citizens and leaders; the increasingly apparent need for serious reform; and the sharpening divisions within Soviet society as the reform process unfolded.

The Afghanistan War Contributed to the Breakdown of the Soviet Union

Rafael Reuveny and Aseem Prakash

In this viewpoint, academics Rafael Reuveny and Aseem Prakash argue that the Afghanistan War was a key cause of the disintegration of the Soviet Union. The war damaged the reputation and the morale of the Soviet army and changed how Soviet leaders viewed the army's usefulness in putting down secessionist movements in non-Russian republics. It weakened the internal unity of both the army and the country and created conditions for the demilitarizing of Soviet society. The war also served to accelerate glasnost (openness) and perestroika (restructing). It gave glasnost and perestroika supporters the opportunity to redefine the relationship between the Soviet people and

SOURCE. Rafael Reuveny and Aseem Prakash, "The Afghanistan war and the breakdown of the Soviet Union," *Review of International Studies*, vol. 25, 1999, pp. 693–708. Copyright © British International Studies Association 1999. Reprinted with the permission of Cambridge University Press and the authors.

the state as well as among the various state organs. Rafael Reuveny is a professor of political economy and environmental policy at Indiana University. Aseem Prakash is a professor of political science at University of Washington, Seattle.

Most scholars typically have viewed the Afghanistan war as a minor and containable conflict that had minimal impact on the basic institutions of the Soviet system. However, we view this war as one of the key causes, along with systemic and leadership-based factors, in the disintegration of the Soviet Union. The repeated failures in this war changed the Soviet leadership's perception of the efficacy of using force to keep non-Soviet nationalities within the Union . . . , devastated the morale and legitimacy of the army . . . , disrupted domestic cohesion . . . , and accelerated *glasnost* [openness]. These effects operated synergistically. War failures weakened the military and conservative anti-reform forces and accelerated *glasnost* and *perestroika* [restructuring]. Importantly, these failures demonstrated that the Soviet army was not invincible, thereby encouraging non-Russian republics to push for independence with little fear of a military backlash. . . .

The Impact on Domestic Politics

The Soviets intervened in Afghanistan in December 1979. . . . Though the Afghanistan war initially was visualized by Soviet leaders as a small-scale intervention, it grew into a decade-long war involving nearly one million Soviet soldiers, killing and injuring some tens of thousands of them. . . .

By late 1986, the Afghanistan war had significantly impacted Soviet domestic politics. Anti-militarism became strong in the non-Russian

> We categorize the war's effects into four types: (1) Perception effects; (2) Military effects; (3) Legitimacy effects; and (4) *Glasnost* effects.

Soviet republics. For non-Russians, the war became a unifying symbol of their opposition to Moscow's rule. The decision to withdraw from Afghanistan signalled Soviet military weakness and demonstrated that the army was vulnerable. By 1988, the war had changed the perceptions of Soviet leaders regarding the efficacy of using military force to hold the disintegrating country together.

This war also discredited the Soviet army. Since the Soviet army was the glue that held the diverse Soviet Republics together, its defeat in Afghanistan had profound implications for the survivability of the Soviet Union. Corruption, looting, and plundering by Soviet soldiers destroyed the army's moral legitimacy. The ethnic split in the army was accentuated when non-Russian soldiers, particularly those from Asian regions, displayed ambivalence toward fighting Afghans, deserted, and even revolted. . . .

Four Categories of Effects

We categorize the war's effects into four types: (1) Perception effects; (2) Military effects; (3) Legitimacy effects; and (4) *Glasnost* effects. These categories are not equally important in explaining the impact of the Afghanistan war on Soviet politics and hence on Soviet breakdown. We consider the Perception and Military effects as being most important followed by Legitimacy effects, and finally *Glasnost* effects.

The Perception and Military effects refer to the discrediting of the Soviet army, perhaps the most important institution for holding the diverse country together, and to the changed Soviet leadership's perception on the efficacy of employing the army to quell secessionist movements in non-Russian republics. In particular, the *Afgantsy* [Afghan War veterans] played a key role in discrediting the army. Legitimacy effects describe the weakening of the army's and the country's internal cohesion. Finally, *Glasnost* effects refer to the impact of the war on accelerating *glasnost* by emboldening the media to report non-official war stories, thereby widening cleavages among various organs of the Soviet state.

Perception Effects

Soviet leaders before Gorbachev believed that they could, and should, employ the military to hold together their diverse country. . . .

From 1979 to 1986, the war was portrayed by the Soviet media and leadership as an 'international duty',

A Bloody Conflict

Since Soviet tanks rolled into Afghanistan in December 1979, an estimated 500,000 people have been killed in a war that has pitted Soviet and Afghan military units against anti-Communist mujahedin guerrillas. . . .

This is a bitter war, one without rules or limits. In early April, according to the mujahedin [Afghan groups opposing the Soviets], the Soviets used poison gas in an attack on guerrilla antiaircraft positions. Hoja Inatullah, 19, says he nearly died of asphyxiation, surviving only by wetting his blanket and breathing through it. "For four or five hours afterward, I had trouble breathing," he says. "My friends carried me to the bomb shelter, and I lay there spitting up black fluid." In such a conflict, justice can be harsh for captured invaders. Said a young guerrilla named Ismail: "We won't shoot them. Bullets are too expensive. Maybe we will stone them to death, or cut their throats, or throw them off a cliff."

SOURCE: *Robert Schultheis and Ken Olsen, "War of a Thousand Skirmishes: Two* Time *Reporters Look at Both Sides of the Afghan Conflict,"* Time *129, no. 20 (May 18, 1987).*

and exercise in 'good neighborliness'. Officially, the war in Afghanistan did not exist. February 1986 marks a turning point in the official portrayal of the war. . . .

As the full story of the war unfolded, Soviet political leaders began distancing themselves from the decision to intervene in Afghanistan. They tried scapegoating the army and 'the geriatric leadership of the previous regime'. . . .

> The army was . . . the glue that held together diverse ethnic groups, primarily because it was perceived as being invincible.

Prior to the Afghanistan war, pro-secession leaders in the non-Russian Soviet republics perceived the Soviet leadership as having the will and the ability to employ the military to crush them. The Afghanistan war changed this perception. Since both the will and the ability of the leadership were under a cloud, non-Russian movements were emboldened to openly preach secession.

To summarize, the Afghanistan war changed the Soviet leaders' perceptions about the efficacy of employing troops to suppress non-Russian secessionist movements. It accentuated ethnic strife within the army, especially the resentment of Asian nationalities towards their being used to suppress their ethnic kin in Afghanistan. As a result, Soviet leaders no longer considered their army to be reliable for suppressing secessionist movements.

Military Effects

In the Soviet Union the security forces, particularly the army, were key players in domestic politics. Due to its heroic role in World War II the Soviet army was a cherished institution. It was a microcosm of the Soviet society, drawing soldiers from diverse nationalities. The army was viewed as the main defender of communism . . . , it was the glue that held together diverse ethnic groups, primarily because it was perceived as being invincible. The army's poor performance in Afghanistan was therefore shocking for soldiers, generals, party cadres, and ordinary citizens. Since the military was an important pillar of the anti-*perestroika* camp, the reverses in Afghanistan weakened anti-reformists, hastened *perestroika*, and facilitated the collapse of the system.

Since a major focus of *perestroika* and *glasnost* was the demilitarization of Soviet society, the war emerged as a rallying point against the military. The poor performance of the Soviet army in Afghanistan and the large number of Soviet casualties fuelled demands to change the military's role. . . .

In late 1989, the Congress of People's Deputies established a commission to inquire into the causes and consequences of the Afghanistan war. Thus, the hallowed institution of the army now had its performance evaluated by a civilian body. The generals, reeling under criticism, joined in this debate. This was unprecedented because in the past the army had seldom felt the need to justify its policies and actions. . . .

These developments adversely affected the army. In late 1989, a poll conducted by the Soviet Ministry of Defence reported a crisis-like environment and unhappiness among army officers. Importantly, as this news was leaked to civilian newspapers, the internal weakness of the army became public knowledge, thereby strengthening the public's perceptions of the army's weakness. . . .

With . . . reports of looting and brutal treatment of Afghan civilians coming in, the army began losing its moral high ground among Soviet citizens. . . .

The Afgantsy

Like any other war, the Afghanistan war crippled and injured soldiers who then had to be sent home. Many *Afgantsy* returned from this war desiring to actively participate in the reorganization of society. By the mid-1980s, there were already about a million *Afgantsy* in the

Soviet Union and they had emerged 'as a new social force in their own right'.

In the early years of the war, the Soviet leadership, wanting to play down Soviet involvement in Afghanistan, did not acknowledge the presence of the *Afgantsy*. The official media ignored them as well. The *Afgantsy* often could not find jobs. Worse still, military authorities provided them with little assistance in obtaining housing and medical care. Many Soviet citizens also had mixed emotions about them; though the *Afgantsy* had fought for the country, they had fought an unpopular war and had committed atrocities on Afghan civilians. . . .

The *Afgantsy* felt betrayed. Many of them organized into vigilante groups determined to fight the money grubbers and 'scroungers' who had sent them to war and were ignoring their existence. By the late 1980s, some *Afgantsy* had begun organizing themselves politically. . . .

Finally, since the *Afgantsy* had directly experienced the war, they played a major role in discrediting the military apparatus. As they also carried hostile feelings against Moscow, *Afgantsy* were recruited in the non-official militia organized by non-Russian secessionist movements.

> The [Afghanistan] war seriously eroded the legitimacy of the Soviet system and encouraged secession by the non-Russian republics.

To summarize: the Afghanistan war created conditions for the demilitarizing of Soviet society. It created a division between the army and the CPSU [Communist Party of the Soviet Union] and between the army and the citizens. The atrocities committed by Soviet soldiers in Afghanistan undermined the legitimacy of the army as a moral institution that safeguarded the oppressed. Finally, the war created a huge mass of *Afgantsy* who returned home with accounts of cruelty and defeat. They also formed non-party organizations that challenged the legitimacy of the CPSU.

Legitimacy Effects

The Soviet Union was an extremely heterogeneous country encompassing diverse nationalities and religions. Many of these groups had histories of warring with each other and with Moscow/St. Petersburg. Though the Soviet system was supposed to be race-blind, it was not so. The non-Russian minorities, Asian as well as European, resented the Russian 'capture' of the system. The Afghanistan war accentuated such resentments, since the non-Russian Soviet republics perceived it as a Russian war fought by non-Russian soldiers. Moreover, they noticed the similarities between the Russian oppression of Afghanistan and of the non-Russian Soviet republics. The war therefore seriously eroded the legitimacy of the Soviet system and encouraged secession by the non-Russian republics. It alienated both elites and masses and gave the secessionist movements a popular rallying cause against Russian domination. . . .

As public opposition to the war increased, it began to infect the local Central Asian party cadres. This development alarmed Moscow and resulted in wide-scale political purges. Though the official media claimed that these purges reflected *perestroika* and the campaigns against corruption, the local population often interpreted them as reflecting Moscow's distrust of local party leadership. This perception was reinforced since ethnic Russians were often the new appointees to these positions. It accentuated the alienation of the Central Asian republics and resulted in riots and civil unrest. . . .

By the late 1980s, the European Soviet republics had begun challenging the Soviet Defence Ministry to decide on their draftees' place of service. Instead of being sent to serve in Afghanistan, they demanded that their draftees serve within their home republic.

To summarize: the Afghanistan war accentuated the cleavages between the non-Russian republics and the Soviet state. It provided a common rallying banner for

the secessionist movements and led to many anti-war demonstrations. In effect, it severely eroded the legitimacy of the Soviet system in the eyes of the non-Russian nationalities.

Glasnost Effects

The impact of the Afghanistan war was so devastating that war reports challenging the official versions could not be suppressed. Importantly, . . . the official media also began showing signs of independence in its war reporting, thereby transforming itself from an outlet for official stories to a barometer of public opinion. . . .

> In the last analysis, it is only dramatic and significant events that cause empires to collapse . . . and the only event that fits this bill is the Afghan war.

We identify four phases in the transformation of media in the Soviet Union. In phase one (1979–80), the central regime strongly censored the media. Accordingly, the media maintained that the Afghanistan war was being fought by the Afghan armed forces, and that the Soviet army was only supporting them from the rear. . . .

In phase two (1981–mid-1985), the media began publishing accounts of the army being actually involved in fighting. . . .

The third phase (mid-1985–89) was heralded by *glasnost*. Beginning in the late 1985, we find a flood of reports and letters to newspapers against the Afghanistan war. . . .

The last stage (1989 onwards) of this transformation covers the time period of the Soviet withdrawal from Afghanistan. In 1989 and the early 1990s, the press routinely carried interviews in which Army generals blamed politicians for engaging in the war in spite of the army's advice to the contrary. In effect, with the Afghanistan war having provided new fuel to *glasnost*, the media began playing an independent role as a watchdog of public interest, a barometer of public opinion, and, more

Photo on previous page: A young Soviet soldier (center) has been captured by the mujahedeen in Afghanistan. Fierce resistance to the Soviet invasion aided in the USSR's demise. (Patrick David/ AFP/Getty Images.)

importantly, an arena of contestations among the various organs of the hitherto unified state.

To summarize: the Afghanistan war provided the supporters of *glasnost* and *perestroika* with a key opportunity for redefining the relationship between the citizens and the Soviet state as well as among the various organs of the state itself. . . .

The Significance of the Afghan War

The disintegration of the Soviet empire started toward the end of the 1980s when Eastern Europe left the Soviet bloc. The Cold War ended in 1989, and in 1991, the Soviet Union itself disintegrated. . . .

Would the Soviet Union have collapsed in the absence of the Afghanistan war? . . .

Systemic factors were undoubtedly important in the decay, though not in the collapse of the Soviet system. . . .

Similarly, the role of Gorbachev and [Soviet Foreign Minister Eduard] Shevardnadze was important in the collapse of the Soviet Union. The war changed their perceptions and those of other Soviet leaders about the efficacy of employing the army to suppress secessionist movements. . . .

Finally, should the Cold War itself be considered as the major war that led to the collapse of the Soviet Union . . . ? In our view—no. In many ways the Cold War is probably better viewed as a chronic problem that was troublesome rather than threatening to the integrity of the USSR. . . . The Soviet Union—in spite of its multiple inefficiencies—was not only able to bear the costs of the Cold War but had to a large degree internalized them. In the last analysis, it is only dramatic and significant events that cause empires to collapse, not ongoing standoffs—and the only event that fits this bill is the Afghan war, perhaps one of the most over-studied but underestimated military conflicts in the history of the twentieth century.

Neither American nor Western Pressure Brought Down the Soviet Union

Jack F. Matlock, Jr.

In the following viewpoint, diplomat Jack F. Matlock, Jr., contends that neither American nor Western pressure brought down the Soviet Union. Ultimately three major separate but interconnected events that took place at the end of the 1980s and ended in 1991—the end of the Cold War, the end of Communist control of the Soviet Union, internal pressures and contradictions—made possible the breakup of the Soviet Union. There is no truth to the three widespread myths that the United States won the Cold War, forced the end of the Cold War through military pressure, and was caught unawares by the Soviet breakup. Jack F. Matlock, Jr., served as American ambassador to the Soviet Union from

SOURCE. Jack F. Matlock, Jr., "in," *The Fifteenth Anniversary of the End of the Soviet Union: Recollections and Perspectives: Occasional Paper #299*, December 13, 2006, pp. 5–8. Copyright © 2006 The Woodrow Wilson International Center for Scholars. All rights reserved. Reproduced by permission.

1987 to 1991 and is the author of a number of books, including *Reagan and Gorbachev: How the Cold War Ended* (1994) and *Autopsy of an Empire: The American Ambassador's Account of the Collapse of the Soviet Union* (1995).

I will address what I consider some of the most damaging and mistaken myths about the breakup of the Soviet Union, because I think that these are widespread. I hope they're not widespread among those of us who really experienced these events, but they are among the public at large. I would like to set them to rest at least in terms of the way I understand things, and understood them at the time. . . .

One has to look at the three seismic events—seismic in geopolitical terms—that occurred right at the end of the 1980s and culminated in 1991. These three events are interconnected, but they were separate events. They had different causes, and the American role in each was quite different.

The End of the Cold War

The first geopolitically seismic event was the end of the Cold War. We can argue about when it ended. I think it ended ideologically in December 1988, but obviously there was still a lot of cleanup diplomacy necessary at that time. I've been accused of belittling it by calling it "cleanup diplomacy." I don't belittle it at all. It was extremely important diplomacy. But certainly by, say, early autumn of 1990, the Cold War was totally over, with all the important issues raised by the Cold War settled. By then, of course, Europe had been united. Germany was united and allowed to stay in NATO [North Atlantic Treaty Organization]—and with Soviet

> "When the Cold War ended, the Soviet system was no longer what it had been."

blessing. Emigration was virtually free at that time from the Soviet Union. That had been a big issue for us. Reform of the Soviet system was proceeding at a dizzying pace, and when Iraq invaded Kuwait, the Soviet Union voted with the United States and others in the Security Council. There was not one significant element of the Cold War left unresolved at that point. The first of these seismic events was in fact the end of the Cold War, and that's one that I think the United States and the Soviet leadership at that time cooperated on.

Former ambassador to the Soviet Union Jack F. Matlock, Jr. dismissed the notion that the United States "won" the Cold War. (**AP Images.**)

One of the myths that we hear—and I think it's very damaging—is that we won the Cold War, as if it was a victory over another country. President [Ronald] Reagan put it much more accurately in his memoirs when he said it was a victory of one system over another. I would add to that: when the Cold War ended, the Soviet system was

How the Cold War Started

When did the Cold War start? The answer is classic irony in the somber shadow of today's headlines. For it started when the President of the United States decided to protect Iran from our wartime ally, the Soviet Union.

The wartime allies had used Iran—with the Soviets occupying northern Iran and the British and American forces occupying the south—as a back-door Allied supply line to the Red [Soviet] Army. At their Teheran Conference in 1943 all the allies had agreed to clear out of Iran within six months of an armistice in Europe.

The Western allies withdrew before that deadline, which was March 6, 1946. The Soviets did not. . . .

So . . . Harry Truman . . . threatened to deploy U.S. naval and ground forces in the Persian Gulf if the Soviets didn't pull the Red Army out of Iran. . . .

During that same spring, it became clear that the Soviets wouldn't abide by the Potsdam agreement that Germany should be treated as an economic unit. The Western allies—Britain, France, and the U.S.—started to consolidate the non-Soviet zones, thus ratifying the de facto division of Germany.

That summer, another crisis brewed. The Soviets proposed to put an end to the international supervision of the Dardanelles [a narrow strait in Northwestern Turkey] and establish Soviet bases in Turkey. Twenty-five divisions of the Red Army were maneuvering near the Turkish border to show they meant it. . . .

Faced with resistance from Turkey and tough U.S. and British diplomacy backed by the aircraft carrier Franklin D. Roosevelt's "courtesy calls" in the Mediterranean, Stalin "stayed his hand" in Turkey—but tightened the screws on Greece.

The climax came when the Greek government, controlling only a "shrunken area" around Athens, appealed for international help. . . . In February, a rigged election put Communists in power in Poland—and another piece of Allied postwar planning, the Yalta agreement, was snuffed out by Soviet noncompliance. . . .

[In] March 1947, with the indispensable help of a senior Republican, Senator Arthur Vandenberg of Michigan, President Truman laid it on the line in a historic address to a joint session of Congress. He called for massive help to both Greece and Turkey. . . .

The great confrontation we came to call the Cold War had quite suddenly become the next stage of world history. What began in Iran in 1946 lasted for 45 years, until the dissolution of the Soviet Union in 1991.

SOURCE: Harlan Cleveland, "The Cold War," keynote address at 2006 symposium, "The Cold War: An Eyewitness Perspective," Washington, DC, October 21, 2006. http://www.archives.gov/research/cold-war/symposium/cleveland.html.

no longer what it had been. In cooperating to end the Cold War, Gorbachev made no concessions that were contrary to the interests of his country. The agreements we made were in the interests of both countries. It was a "win-win" solution, and it freed the Soviet Union of the burden of the arms race, which was really killing it. There was cooperation, and both sides won. It was the communist system and the old policies that lost, but they were changing already.

The End of Communist Control in the Soviet Union

The second big change—and this didn't occur overnight, but it occurred very rapidly—was the end of communist control over the Soviet Union, ultimate communist control. Now this was not done by Western pressure. I'm a great admirer of President Reagan and his diplomacy . . . but he was not the man who defeated communism. The man who defeated communism in the Soviet Union was Mikhail Gorbachev. As general secretary, he was probably the only person who could have done it, by forcing or tricking the party and the *nomenklatura* [ruling bureaucratic elite] to take themselves out of ultimate control of the country. It was these two events, the end of the Cold War and the end of communist control of the Soviet Union, that eventually made the breakup of the Soviet Union possible. It broke up, I think, entirely because of internal pressures, internal contradictions. That would not have happened, in my judgment, if the Cold War had still been raging. Under those conditions, Gorbachev could not have embarked on his *perestroika* [economic and government restructuring policy], and without *perestroika* the Communist Party and the organs of repression it controlled would

> I think the idea that we somehow forced the Soviet collapse is the opposite of the truth.

have prevented the Soviet republics from seceding and destroying the Soviet state.

The Myth of U.S. Military Pressure

The Cold War had served to contain tensions in the Soviet Union as a pressure cooker contains steam. This helped keep the Soviet Union intact. It helped keep the Communist Party in control. When the Cold War ended, this created an entirely new situation. The idea that American or Western pressure brought down the Soviet Union seems to me utterly absurd. It turns reality on its head. And this attitude is quite dangerous: it led to triumphalism in the 1990s and the idea that Russia should be treated as a defeated power. Actually, Russia wasn't even a party to the Cold War. It was only one part—though the largest part—of the Soviet Union.

Now related to that is the myth that somehow the U.S. forced the end of the Cold War through military pressure. In fact, I recall that during the first Reagan administration, when I drafted guidance for government officials, I included instructions not to question the legitimacy of the Soviet government. We did not ask for regime change, we asked for a change of behavior, particularly a change of behavior externally. Our military buildup was meant to back up our diplomacy, not to give Gorbachev an easy way out, knowing that he really needed to reduce the defense burden, but to encourage him to open up the country and reform simultaneously. This, I believe, was in the ultimate interest of the Soviet Union, if it could have been kept together at all. So I think the idea that we somehow forced the Soviet collapse is the opposite of the truth. And frankly, that perception, which many people have, has led us into some very serious foreign policy blunders.

> "We in the American embassy in Moscow saw what was happening. We did not want it to happen the way it did."

U.S. Awareness and Understanding

A third myth I will mention is that the U.S. was caught unawares. It's usually said that this must be true because the CIA [Central Intelligence Agency] never predicted the breakup of the Soviet Union. That's true. Thank goodness the CIA never officially predicted the breakup, because the moment they did, if they had, it would have leaked, and the whole process of reform in the Soviet Union would have ended. But the fact that the U.S. intelligence community refrained from a formal prediction that the Soviet Union would destroy itself doesn't mean our policymakers didn't understand what was going on. As ambassador to the Soviet Union, I sent my first message that advised the United States government to make contingency plans for the possible breakup of the Soviet Union in June 1990, 18 months before it happened. My "heads-up" was not based upon clandestine intelligence. . . .

I think our embassy understood much better what was happening in the country than Gorbachev did himself, because the KGB [Soviet secret police] was giving him false information.

There is another lesson here that some people seem to have forgotten. When you insist upon hearing only what you want to hear, you usually don't get the true picture. So yes, we in the American embassy in Moscow saw what was happening. We did not want it to happen the way it did. Of course we wanted the three Baltic countries to recover their independence. We would have been very happy to see Gorbachev negotiate a voluntary union treaty of the remaining 12 republics.

As a matter of fact, when President [George H.W.] Bush the elder, on August 1, 1991, in Kyiv, made a speech that Bill Safire jokingly called "the Chicken Kiev speech," it was supposed to be for all the non-Russian republics, not just Ukraine. What he said was "don't confuse freedom with independence." Freedom first. Although Bush did not explain in detail, what he had in mind was that if a republic became part of a federal, democratic state, they could, if they had good cause later, secede. If, however, they declared independence before they had a democratic system, freedom might be harder to obtain. . . .

Next Steps: Democratic Movements and Independence

So, the fact is that the United States did not engineer the Soviet collapse; we did what we could to encourage a democratizing Soviet Union. Obviously we had no influence over the situation by the summer of 1991 because internal forces, aided by some of Gorbachev's mistakes, were what was forcing the country apart.

I would just add one thing, and that is that many people cheered when the Soviet Union collapsed, thinking this is the end of problems, that suddenly everything was going to be sweetness and light and so on. When I wrote a book on the collapse of the Soviet Union, *Autopsy on an Empire*—it was published in 1995—I said my champagne is still corked because we didn't know what's going to happen. The problem was that in Gorbachev's last years it was Moscow that was giving great support to the democratic movements in many of the other republics. I had a Belarusian tell me, "When our local officials would not let me publish my things, I would go to the Central Committee in Moscow, and they would order them to be published." I talked in 1991 to democratic forces in Uzbekistan, Tajikistan, Kyrgyzstan, and so on. Now almost all of these forces have been virtually wiped out, and they went very quickly.

Often I think that the regional parties, the republic party leaders, saw that Gorbachev's reforms were going to undermine their power, and chose independence in order to maintain their power. So as we look back, I think it is important, as we remember those days, to think about what really happened, and to reconsider the lessons we might have drawn from them.

The Commonwealth of Independent States May Disintegrate

Vladislav Dobkov

In the following viewpoint, Vladislav Dobkov claims that unless the three leaders of the former Soviet republics of Russia, Ukraine, and Belarus who founded the Commonwealth of Independent States (CIS) find a way soon to put aside their differences and self-interests and achieve real cooperation, the CIS will fall apart. Their aversion to Soviet president Mikhail Gorbachev and the Soviet Union appears to have been their only unifying factor. As soon as they got out from under his supervision, their relationship began to disintegrate. Mistrust, personal disagreements and ambitions, lack of resolution to issues raised at summits held to date, and the continuing breakdown of the former Soviet Union all pose a serious threat to the organization's future. Vladislav Dobkov is the U.S. correspondent for *Pravda*, until 1991 a publication of the Communist Party and the leading newspaper of the former Soviet Union.

SOURCE. Vladislav Dobkov, "Does the Fate of the Soviet Union Await the Commonwealth of Independent States?" *Demokratizatsiya*, vol. 1, 1993, pp. 48–54. Copyright © 1993. Reprinted with permission of the Helen Dwight Reid Educational Foundation.

> Their positions on nearly all problems of the Commonwealth are drifting farther and farther apart, exposing the yawning abyss among these former Soviet republics.

History's nasty habit of repeating past tragedies in the form of a modernized farce threatens to confirm itself in the destiny of the Commonwealth of Independent States (CIS).

This knowingly shaky and hurriedly tailored formation appeared on the ruins of the old Soviet Union in December of 1991 due to the efforts of three leaders of former Soviet republics—the presidents of Russia and Ukraine, and the chairman of the Supreme Soviet of Belarus. Boris Yeltsin, Leonid Kravchuk and Stanislav Shushkevich were eager to rid themselves, as soon as possible, of the center's guardianship which was embodied in Soviet President Mikhail Gorbachev and in Moscow's power structures. Their feeling was so burning and unanimous, that these three extremely different and contradictory politicians decided to undertake joint action; and at first, they even demonstrated a great deal of mutual understanding and cooperation.

Alas, the events of recent months have shown that their dislike for Gorbachev and the Soviet Union had been the strongest, if not the only, unifying factor in the behavior of these key CIS figures. Their positions on nearly all problems of the Commonwealth are drifting farther and farther apart, exposing the yawning abyss among these former Soviet republics. The fact of the matter is that their opposition to Gorbachev was the catalyst which made them become the founding fathers of the CIS. Their goal was opposition to the center. As soon as they (the three members of the former Politburo of the CPSU [Communist Party of the Soviet Union] Central Committee) got rid of their former General Secretary's guardianship . . . their inveterate mistrust, new ambitions and grievances began to distance them farther away from each other.

Differing Aspirations, Personal Ambitions, and Incompatability

Even a fleeting glance at the map of the former Soviet Union is sufficient to make two basic facts certain: 1) the three republics which caused the collapse of the Union and laid the foundation for the creation of the CIS are decisively different according to their "weight" and influence within this new formation; 2) they are the closest of neighbors, which have their economic infrastructures intertwined to such an extent that they are, in fact, doomed to cooperation and mutual understanding.

This opposing dualism of the current position of these three independent states is a destabilizing factor in their interrelationships. On the one hand, the influence of Moscow, Kiev and Minsk has to be equal according to

Russian President Boris Yeltsin (4th from left) shakes hands with Ukranian President Leonid Kravchuk during the family photo of the CIS leaders at a summit meeting in Minsk. Self-interest on the part of Russia, Ukraine, and Belarus brought the former Soviet states together. (**Janek Skarzynski/AFP/Getty Images.**)

the declared principles of existence of the CIS as a voluntary union of states which enjoy equal rights. On the other hand, the unequal potential of these republics, the differences of their aspirations, and the objective incompatibility of their national interests all keep them from acting together. Finally, unilateral actions taken by any of them have immediate influence on their neighbors.

In addition, true and imaginary mutual grievances and old scores do not allow these three leaders to work together towards the achievement of common ground on a growing number of concrete problems. But this is not all. As the actions of Ukrainian President Kravchuk . . . have illustrated, these leaders' personal ambitions and their power struggle to lead the CIS might seriously undermine all attempts to establish effective interaction within the Commonwealth. As a result, the escape from excessive guardianship of the center has not brought the republics together, but pushed them apart. In the course of just a few months, many of the connections between them have been broken. . . .

A Counterproductive Rivalry: Russia and Ukraine

And thus, Ukraine and Russia are dividing their belongings, foreign holdings included, like spouses separating after an unhappy marriage. For example, they are unable to agree on the mutual supply of oil and treasury notes, grain, fertilizers, etc. The most outstanding of these absurdities is the attempt by Kiev and Moscow to divide the Black Sea Fleet. Neither of them, in fact, need this fleet unless they intend to compete with the United States over the control of the Mediterranean. . . . Moreover, its maintenance threatens to become an inordinately large burden for the ruined economies of both republics. . . .

The two presidents, at the last minute, decided to postpone a solution to the problem until better times. And then finally, on June 23, 1992, Yeltsin and Kravchuk met in Dagomys [microdistrict of Sochi, Russia] and decided to keep the Black Sea Fleet under unified command. . . .

The Commonwealth in Peril

The clash of unsatisfied ambitions of the leaders currently in power in Moscow and Kiev is extremely reminiscent of the struggle by members of the old party and economic *nomenklatura* [ruling bureaucratic elite]. This struggle undermined the unity of the USSR long before its disintegration. The same slogans (only with a "democratic" slant), the same methods, the same appeals to nationalistic prejudice manifest themselves in the current struggle.

> 'If the situation does not change, the Commonwealth is doomed.'

In November of 1991 Yeltsin, Kravchuk and Shushkevich gathered secretly in the picturesque reserve of Belovezhskaya Pushcha. . . . There, like a lured wild boar who had lost his vigilance, the Soviet Union was shot down. They hardly conceived the fact that their hastily created Commonwealth might fall victim to acute disagreements between the two leading participants of the deal. Belarus, which always tried to avoid quarrels with either of its more powerful neighbors, could not or did not want to play the role of mediator between them. And so the Ukrainian-Russian disagreements, heated by the rivalry of the two leaders, began to consistently destroy the newly created Commonwealth.

In March 1992, a meeting of states and governments of the CIS was held. It was there, in Kiev, that this destructive work produced its first results. Practically all the questions put on the meeting agenda . . . were left unresolved. . . . After the conclusion of the CIS summit in Kiev, the Ukrainian president did not hide his skeptical attitude towards the Commonwealth's prospects. He stated, "If the situation does not change, the Commonwealth is doomed."

The Failure at Tashkent

The situation had changed by the time of the May meeting in Tashkent; it was a change for the worse. These former Soviet republics failed to find ways to resolve most of the common problems facing them. The demarcation between the two leading CIS states, Russia and Ukraine, had gone even farther and the fate of the Black Sea Fleet had not been determined at that time. Kravchuk, who went to Washington on the eve of the meeting, agreed to continue the transfer of strategic nuclear weapons to Russian territory, but only due to pressure from the Americans. Russia began to create its own army (the CIS architects earlier supposed that this would not happen), and Yeltsin appointed himself its commander-in-chief. On top of all this, Kravchuk did not show up at the meeting in Tashkent at all. His example was followed by the leaders of three other CIS states—Moldova, Kyrgyzstan, and Tajikistan. Only six of the eleven Commonwealth countries joined the defense union, which replaced the past security guarantees provided by the USSR. Moreover, one of these republics, Armenia, at the conclusion of the Tashkent agreement was basically at war with Azerbaijan, over the Nagorno-Karabakh region. . . . As in Kiev, the Tashkent meeting participants failed to create any effective mechanism for processing and solving Commonwealth problems. . . . Instead of moving closer together after the Tashkent meeting, the CIS members started to float farther apart. . . .

The Continuing Breakdown: Cause for Concern

In my view, the main threat to the future of the CIS comes not only from the personal disagreements and ambitions of its largest participants' leaders or from the modest results of the summits held so far, but also from the continuing breakdown of the former Soviet Union.

The centrifugal [outward] tendencies released by the Belovezhskaya Pushcha deal . . . are far from settling down. An example is the declaration of independence by Tatarstan, which was earlier a part of Russia. Analogous steps are being taken by the representative powers in Crimea. . . . Even earlier, independence from Russia was declared by Chechenia. . . .

In the Dniester region (which is still a part of Moldova) ethnic Russians are unwilling to stay under the control of this republic's authorities, who are aiming at unification with Romania. Military actions have been going on there for a long time, and threaten to grow into another "local" civil war. By the end of June 1992, the self-declared independent Dniester region became extremely explosive; Moldovan troops were shelling Bendery, a Russian secessionist stronghold. Yeltsin threatened to use military force in order to defend the local, predominantly Russian population. In the Moldovan Parliament, it was concluded that their small republic . . . was at an undeclared state of war with Russia. If the worst happens, Russia will find itself fighting another member of the CIS, only several months after its creation. . . .

Unfortunately in most cases, the response of today's democratic central authorities in regard to the expressions of dissent in the provinces appears to be no better than that of the old Party administrative stereotypes. . . . Thus, the process of demarcation and breakup of the former Soviet Union is far from over. It might pose yet more surprises to the CIS leaders and the outside world. And these surprises, I am afraid, will not all be pleasant.

An Urgent Need for Real Cooperation

It is hard to tell how long the CIS can exist under these conditions. Mikhail Gorbachev stated recently at a press conference in Washington that if the CIS initiators did not manage to achieve real cooperation among the former Soviet republics soon, the world would hear more bad news about the breakup of economic ties, collapse of the banking system, armed forces' disagreements, territorial arguments and violations of human and minority rights.

I have not agreed with Mikhail Sergeevich Gorbachev for a long time now. I must agree, however, with his assessment of the prospective developments in the CIS. If the organizers and main actors of the Commonwealth of Independent States fail to immediately come to agreement about the forms and methods of its functioning, they, at least, need to address the most urgent tasks. They include: restoring broken ties, developing contacts among the republics, ceasing petty arguments and the parading of national selfishness. If the organizers fail to do this, the CIS is threatened with the same fate that befell the Soviet Union in December 1991.

A fast and painful disintegration awaits the Commonwealth of Independent States.

The Commonwealth of Independent States May Endure for Some Time

John Gray

In this viewpoint, written in 1992, John Gray agrees with Ukraine president Leonid Kravchuk that in essence the Commonwealth of Independent States is a way to control the collapse of the Soviet Union. For more than 70 years, no republic was allowed to function on its own. The republics and their citizens were bound together by the inflexible rules of the Communist Party and the Soviet state. When the Soviet Union fell, there was a need to create something to take its place. The Commonwealth filled that need. Its members are "chained by the links of the past." Until new ties are built, the Commonwealth is likely to continue to exist in one form or another. John Gray has worked for a number of Canadian newspapers, including the *Globe and Mail*, where he has served as Ottawa bureau chief, national editor, foreign editor, foreign correspondent, and national correspondent.

SOURCE. John Gray, "Chained Together by the Past," *The Globe and Mail*, March 27, 1992, p. A21. Copyright © 1992 Globe Interactive, a division of Bell Globemedia Publishing, Inc. Reproduced by permission.

The Russian word for Commonwealth is *sodrujestvo*, which also carries the meaning of concord, co-operation and friendship among nations.

It is a nice idea, this friendship among nations. But the assumption now is that when they were creating the Commonwealth of Independent States out of the remains of the Soviet Union a few months ago, they were carried away more by the poetry than the reality.

Of friendship, co-operation and concord, there is little evidence among the 11 members of the Commonwealth of Independent States. If they gather in the same room once a month, it is only because that seems a practical thing to do—and there are even doubts about that.

The Unresolved Dilemma of the Commonwealth

For more than 70 years, the people of the Union of Soviet Socialist Republics were bound together by the iron rules of the Communist Party and the Soviet state. Whoever and wherever you were, someone in Moscow decided your life—what language you should learn, what gods you should not worship, how many loaves of bread would be produced by your local baker.

Over the whole vast area, one-sixth of the world's land mass, an incredibly complex economic system ensured that each region was linked to every other. No republic could stand alone.

> There is undoubtedly a core of hardline Communists who would like to recreate the Soviet Union.

Not surprisingly, when the Soviet Union finally collapsed in December [1991], the event was greeted by two distinctly opposite reactions.

One was to say good riddance.

The other was to assume that getting rid of the Soviet Union was all very well, but something had to be created to take its place. Those two positions are the unresolved dilemma of the Commonwealth.

PARTICIPATING COUNTRIES OF THE COMMONWEALTH OF INDEPENDENT STATES

Area (in square miles)	
Armenia	11,500
Azerbaijan	33,428
Belarus	80,150
Georgia	26,900
Kazakhstan	1,050,000
Kyrgyzstan	76,600
Moldova	13,000
Russia	6,591,100
Tajikistan	55,251
Turkmenistan	188,455
Ukraine	232,046
Uzbekistan	173,552

Date Joined	
December 3, 1991	
December 8, 1991	
December 21, 1991	

*As a result of a conflict in South Ossetia, Georgia withdrew from the Commonwealth on August 14, 2008.

Taken from: *The Columbia Encyclopedia*, Sixth Edition, NY: Columbia University Press, 2008.

There is undoubtedly a core—perhaps a dangerous core—of hardline Communists who would like to recreate the Soviet Union. . . .

There are probably more, but still a minority, who have a certain nostalgia either for what they fancied to be

Central Asia's Dilemma

Few peoples of the world have ever been forced to become independent nations. Yet that is precisely what happened to the five Central Asian republics after Russia, Belarus and Ukraine . . . met in Minsk on December 8, 1991, and created a new Commonwealth of Independent States (CIS).

That action by the three Slavic presidents left Central Asian leaders with an unpleasant choice: they could go it alone—either singly or as a group—or they could shrug off the intended snub by their Slavic counterparts and agree to join the Commonwealth. After a hurried meeting in Ashkhabad, Turkmenistan's capital, they chose the latter course. If independence had to occur, it was best achieved gradually; the new Commonwealth structures, they conceded, would make it easier to regulate their interdependent economies. . . .

Each republic, for the first time, had full control of its own natural resources and local economic enterprises. . . .

Each president headed a country whose economy was still fully intertwined with those of its neighbors. Only the U.S.S.R. had collapsed. Its interregional economic links, though

the ideals of the Communist Party, or for the grandeur of their status as citizens of a superpower. But they know those days are done.

Mikhail Gorbachev: Missing the Point

And then there is Mikhail Gorbachev, the man who changed the world and who in the days of his dwindling power as president of the Soviet Union made himself faintly ridiculous by his obsession with saving a union that was clearly doomed, and rightly so.

Mr. Gorbachev is still at it. "Society is not happy with the disintegration of the country," he says. "People cannot accept that. Those who claim that the country had disappeared are lying. The country abides."

Mr. Gorbachev is wrong in underestimating the swelling hatred for the Communist Party last summer.

damaged, still remained: southern Kazakhstan still got its electricity from Kyrgyzstan, while northern Kazakhstan helped service Siberia's energy grid; Turkmenistan still sent part of its oil to Russia to be made into jet fuel, but it processed Siberian oil in its own refineries. While each new nation continued to depend on its neighbors' basic inputs—fuel, energy and raw materials—the coordinating structures that regulated such commerce shrank or entirely disappeared.

As Soviet central structures withered, so too did subsidies from Moscow that had long helped feed Central Asia's ever increasing population. The region's leaders were left with sole responsibility for keeping their economies afloat. . . .

Nationhood was reluctantly accepted. It has carried with it enormous burdens—mostly economic for which none of the region's leaders could have been prepared and which even the most able consistently tried to avoid.

SOURCE: Martha Brill Olcott, "Central Asia's Catapult to Independence," Foreign Affairs 71, no. 3 (Summer 1992), pp. 108–130.

He is wrong now in underestimating the contempt for a system that has brought a once-proud people to penury and international humiliation.

Yet he is prepared to hector the Commonwealth leaders for their casual approach to the task of building Commonwealth institutions. "Under current conditions, when all old ties are being destroyed, it is necessary to meet at least once a week, or even to stay in one room until agreements are reached," he says.

Lack of Resolution

Mr. Gorbachev misses the point. The evidence of recent months is that the leaders of the Commonwealth do not want the ties so cherished by him and so vital to the Soviet Union. If they wanted the ties, they would not have destroyed the USSR.

The Commonwealth was far from harmonious, failing to resolve internal strife such as the ongoing conflict between Armenia and Azerbaijan over Nagorno-Karabakh. Here, an Aberzaijani woman cries over the death of her son in the conflict. (**AP Images.**)

Take their meeting in Kiev last Friday [March 20, 1992]. By any measure it was a signal failure.

The Commonwealth leaders were faced by a number of problems that had been building for weeks or months. There is a crisis over the disposal of nuclear weapons and a crucial problem over the division of the massive Soviet military establishment.

Who will control the Black Sea Fleet? Which forces are strategic, which conventional? What contribution will the participating states make to the Commonwealth armed forces?

How are Soviet assets, at home and abroad, to be divided? How is the air space over the Commonwealth to be controlled? Will there be a Commonwealth television system?

Is trade among the Commonwealth members to be subject to customs? Will there be controls to stop one Commonwealth country suddenly exploding the price of a vital commodity such as natural gas for other members, as Turkmenistan did for Ukraine?

A hospital in Armenia always bought filters for kidney dialysis machines from Belarus (formerly Byelorussia); [is it] reasonable for the Belarus enterprise now to charge dollars when the hospital has only rubles?

Between two of the Commonwealth states, Armenia and Azerbaijan, an undeclared war has been flaring for four years over the fate of the disputed enclave of Nagorno-Karabakh. Almost 2,000 people have died in the terrible little conflict.

But about Nagorno-Karabakh and a brewing civil war in Moldova, and all the problems cited above, the Kiev meeting did nothing. The Commonwealth heads of state adjourned at 7 o'clock and went home, promising to meet again in five or six weeks.

Mixed Views About the Future

Leonid Kravchuk, President of Ukraine, probably got it right a few weeks ago when he said that the Commonwealth is essentially a way to control the collapse of the Soviet Union. It is a way of bringing civilized procedures to a divorce.

Of all the Commonwealth leaders, Mr. Kravchuk is least enthusiastic about the institution. President Yeltsin of Russia sees it as a way to enlarge the empire of Moscow, because Russia, by its size and richness, will always be the most powerful force. Mr. Kravchuk comes to the same conclusion, and he wants no part of it.

He said after the Kiev meeting that he sees no future for the Commonwealth—there are too many disparate interests, particularly Russian and Ukrainian. "I do not see it. Not because Kravchuk is bad or because Yeltsin is bad. It is an objective process at work."

Some people are prepared to predict the demise of the Commonwealth in perhaps just a few months. It may not come that quickly. The states of Central Asia are looking southward to build ties long prevented by Moscow; the European states are looking westward towards Europe. It takes time.

Those new ties may come eventually, but in the meantime the former republics are chained by the links of the past. As a matter of convenience, the Commonwealth may endure in some form for quite a while. But it will not be loved, and there will never be a Commonwealth anthem to make any heart skip a beat.

CHAPTER 3

Personal Narratives

A Moscow Teen Talks About Perestroika and Glasnost

Yelena, as quoted in Deborah Adelman

In the following viewpoint, a Russian teenager named Yelena shares her feelings about the changes she has experienced because of the reform policies of perestroika (restructuring) and glasnost (openness). She describes an unofficial rally she attended—her first rally ever—and the excitement she felt about people feeling free to voice their opinions without fear of punishment. She admits that perestroika is not perfect and that the economy is in a sad state with food in short supply and industry and the cooperatives in trouble. She knows perestroika has its shortcomings, but she is hopeful that it will be a success because she believes it might really be able to change people's lives for the better. In the spring of 1989 Yelena was a 16-year-old living in Moscow.

Photo on previous page: Moscow citizens used various means of impeding Soviet troops near Red Square during the August 19, 1991 coup. (**AP Images.**)

W hat's going on now should excite people. They can speak out, say what's on their mind, express their positions, and now that we have this opportunity we mustn't let it slip by. But people of our age right now—well, there is really very little we can do; we still know very little about this life of ours.

Preparing for Change

We're preparing ourselves! We're beginning to think differently for ourselves. As it turns out, teachers are playing a very small role in this. Our teachers are there only so that we learn their subject, and that's all. I don't know about my parents. I do talk to my father about what's going

> It seems to me that we are the ones who have to prepare ourselves for something different.

on, and he thinks that if what's going on now doesn't just wither away and develops further, then maybe we'll be able to say that our government isn't completely rotten. But he thinks that his generation can't really change very much. They've gotten used to it, they grew up in such an atmosphere of silence, and it's the most difficult for them to make a transition to a new life. It seems to me that we are the ones who have to prepare ourselves for something different. . . .

This is where perestroika [restructuring] begins: people simply have started to reflect upon our past and about things they didn't question before and didn't know. Before they used to shout about how everything in the Soviet Union was fine and somewhere in another country things were bad. Now everybody understands that's not the way things are; things aren't as simple as they used to say.

The Sad State of the Economy

No matter which direction you look these days, the picture is pretty sorry. Our economy in any sector of production is in a deplorable state. Take industry, for example, all you have to do is simply stop in at a grocery store. We in Moscow are in a state of horror when we go into the shops, but if you compare us with other cities in the Russian federation, things aren't so bad here. Moscow is actually very well supplied because at least we can manage to buy some things, but in other places people have ration cards for meat; they get half a kilo of sausage per person per month. I don't know how to explain that to an American: *one half-kilo of boiled sausage per person per month.* There are terrible articles being written now by workers from other places who stand at their machines, eight hours at an open-hearth furnace, big strong men, and they get half a kilo of sausage a month. They simply don't get any more meat. The meat situation is really bad in other places.

Look, it turns out that there are some regions in the Russian federation, near the Ukraine, southern regions, that send us all they produce—grain for bread, meat, milk—and they themselves are left with nothing and go hungry. . . . I know this because I have relatives who live in those kinds of cities, and when I go there to visit them I am horrified by what they have in their stores. If there is anything, it's only in the cooperatives. Sausage from the cooperatives, canned goods, three times as expensive. And people buy it! . . .

The cooperatives have been a mistake in perestroika. We've already understood that without cooperatives our industry is going to have a hard time. They already passed a law on individual labor. . . . The principle of cooperatives now is that they are supposed to compete with each other and above all with government enterprises, but the way it's turned out there's no competition, just outrageous prices, and the quality is certainly not improving. So

> A lot has changed in these four years, even if only that we can say whatever we want and not be afraid.

now we've ended up with cooperatives that don't actually compete with the government, as well as a market and rackets and everything else imaginable to boot! . . .

Freedom to Speak Out: An Unofficial Rally

I was at a rally yesterday [spring 1989] for the first time in my life, and the most important thing is that it was an unofficial one in which very many good and bold ideas were expressed. But my first impressions were not very good. That rally went on for two hours, but everything was clear after five minutes. Most of the time went to shouting, "Yeltsin! Yeltsin!" "Down with the Committee!" and so on. That mass of people staring into the mouths of those speakers made a bad impression on me. And the mood of that crowd was such that if anybody had said anything against Yeltsin, even one word, they would have torn him to pieces. If they would have told them to storm the office of the Moscow Council, that crowd would have stormed it. Of course I'm glad the meeting happened, and even though there were some real firebrands there, people basically behaved themselves well and eventually dispersed peacefully. The police behaved well. I'm for this way of expressing oneself, because other ways don't lead anywhere. . . .

They've really been after poor Yeltsin. I remember Yeltsin from when he was mayor of the city. They took him from that position, but he managed to do quite a lot for Moscow, little cafes appeared, little stores, they constructed the Arbat pedestrian area, they rebuilt parts of the city, and they got rid of him. And that got people upset. They got rid of Yeltsin—and people already loved him—and now they've formed some commission, and then he was nominated as a candidate [for people's deputy] and they've formed a committee again, using the names of some anonymous workers, and when they tried to verify those addresses it turned out they didn't even exist. How vile! Our leadership should be ashamed. Once again they won't get to the bottom of this and give us evidence about who is guilty. So much for truth in the newspapers!

Glasnost in Action

A lot has changed in these four years, even if only that we can say whatever we want and not be afraid. That rally we were at yesterday shows that. People gathered unofficially, nobody was hassled, and the Moscow Party leadership—the most bureaucratic organization in the city—said nothing. The fact of that meeting is evidence that we have achieved something. Both in the press and on television they broadcast and write about things they would never have talked about before. . . .

They've been showing the election campaign on television, how they're elected first at the workplace. They've been showing all their yammering—I don't know what other word to use to describe it—all their fights and scandals, they interrupt each other at those meetings, get up on the podium so they can start talking themselves, and slander the person who just spoke before them. This doesn't make a very good impression. It's good they're showing it to us, but I don't like the way it's happening.

What I'm learning affects the way I think about my country, but it's hard to say how. The fact that they're talking about all of this is good. The most important thing is for them not to stop talking about all of this now. On the contrary, everybody should be given access to archives and documents.

Cautious Hope for the Future

It's hard to determine now what really corresponds to the truth because we can't form our opinion even about one lecture now, or one article in a newspaper, because they all contradict each other. It's very hard to form an opinion. We have to dig deeper.

I'm counting on the success of perestroika. I want to hope for it. . . . But when [Soviet premier Nikita] Khrushchev came to power he put an end to the personality cult at the Twentieth Party Congress, and it seemed as if it had become possible

> Of course I hope perestroika will triumph, but just hoping isn't very much.

to say anything, but then, gradually . . . well, now they're starting to say that there were two Khrushchevs, the one that emerged at first and then another one, after a few years in power. Everything began to be closed off again, people weren't allowed to speak the truth. . . . This is why I am cautious about our present perestroika and how it's going to end up. Of course I hope perestroika will triumph, but just hoping isn't very much. I don't think my parents believe it will work. They don't say that, but I can feel that they don't believe it will be successful. Four years have already gone by since [Mikhail] Gorbachev became general secretary, and nothing here has changed in our economy.

At home, the minute the news program *Vremya* appears on the TV screen we always watch it, and any time Gorbachev is on we watch him too, but not the way we did during his first years in office. We've already stopped taking it so seriously, and I think he talks a lot. Of course, it's clear why . . . but still, he should talk less. He needs to demand more. Our people are such that if you don't demand anything from them, if you allow them everything, well, you could end up destroying everything good, destroying what's begun. And I don't think he's very demanding.

But even if they are saying that perestroika has its shortcomings, basically everybody is getting swept up in it. They're being inspired by what's going on now here. That's probably the right thing, because the process that's going on here now might really be able to change our lives quite a bit. And they're starting to show us that life needs to be changed, even though I think we knew it before and saw that there's nothing in the stores, we saw that and we didn't need newspapers to tell us that we were living poorly.

A Moscow Professor Takes Part in a Coup

Aleksei Kozhevrikov

In the following viewpoint, written to a friend in the United States in an August 22, 1991, e-mail, Aleksei Kozhevrikov relates how the people of Moscow have come together to defend the Russian parliament during a three-day coup and what transpired as a result. He describes how he participated—the first night in the defense line and the second going around displaying a sign asking soldiers to connect with the crowd on friendly terms. He tells how he watched as a boy attacking a vehicle from the rear was shot to death at point blank range by someone in the vehicle and goes on to describe the reactions of the crowd and the soldiers. He explains that things have quieted down, but the outcome is not known for certain yet. Dr. Aleksei Kozhevrikov is a faculty member at the Institute for the History of Science and Technology of the Academy of Sciences in Moscow.

SOURCE. Aleksei Kozhevrikov, *Russia at the Barricades: Eyewitness Accounts of the August 1991 Coup.* Armonk, NY: M.E. Sharpe Inc., 1994. Copyright © 1994 by M.E. Sharpe, Inc. All rights reserved. Used by permission of M.E. Sharpe, Inc. Not for reproduction.

The general situation is the following. Muscovites are defending the huge building of the Russian parliament right near the American Embassy. There are many politicians inside who organize the opposition, including [Boris] Yeltsin, members of two parliaments—Soviet and Russian—and others. The first night there were about 10,000 people around the building. Yesterday noon there was a large rally with maybe 300,000 people if not more. And last night probably more than 50,000 were constantly staying in defense. Half of them were highly organized: they were divided into detachments and stood in lines close to each other around the walls and on the nearest barricades. Another half were sitting or moving around. There are many armored vehicles in various parts of Moscow. They move in complicated ways and no one, at least outside the building, understands clearly the military situation.

> The second night I went around carrying a placard with a call to soldiers for fraternization.

The radio announcements and rumors are contradictory and not very reliable. Soldiers, when spoken to, do not express readiness to fight with people. Most probably, some troops refused to fight and left the city, but new ones are coming. Two small detachments of tanks and armored vehicles came to the building to help in defense. Besides these places with troops—some blocks in the center of the city and around the parliament building—the rest of the city is quiet and ordinary life goes on. Although a curfew was proclaimed, it is not respected at all.

August 20: A Small Battle

I stayed in the defense line the first night. The second night I went around carrying a placard with a call to soldiers for fraternization. The idea was to meet possible troops earlier and speak to them—everybody was expecting a confrontation this night—even before they reached the major defenses. It turned out that this night [Tuesday, August 20] there were relatively few troops in Moscow, since many left the city in the evening.

I guess that the small battle that took place happened unintentionally at about 1:00 A.M. A small detachment of armored vehicles most probably was not trying to storm the building, but was passing by via Tchaikovsky Street (the one with the American Embassy), about 300 meters from the parliament building. There were barricades on this street at the two entrances of the tunnel. Some vehicles were stopped peacefully (I saw two, maybe there were a few more). Five of them decided to pass through and they got into the tunnel rather easily. I did not watch this, but reportedly there was some shooting into the air. The second barricade was larger. There were some trolleys across the tunnel entrance, and finally the vehicles could not make a hole in it and they were blocked inside. They stopped at a place, about a hundred meters long, with the tunnel entrance at one end, the barricade at the other, and walls (one to five meters high) on their left and right sides.

About three hundred people, including myself, rushed to the place where they heard shooting. When I came close, five vehicles were near the barricade and about two dozen people came down close to them. The soldiers were not very aggressive. In three vehicles they opened the hatches and looked out from them so that the people could speak to them. The defenders who came to the barricades were not an organized detachment but a kind of crowd. Some people behaved peacefully, I too came down to the vehicles with my placard and spoke to the soldiers. Some others (mostly teenagers) were excited and psychologically ready to fight, and

> The vehicle continued moving back and forth, people were still attacking it, and those standing on the walls started screaming 'Murderers!'

Before violence erupted, some people made friendly appeals to soldiers during the August 1991 coup. (AP Images.)

their words and gestures may have looked aggressive and unpleasant to the soldiers.

Death of a Boy

Things quickly became more dangerous when one of the vehicles with closed hatches began to move, actively trying to throw off a man or two who stood on its armored top. A dozen boys were running around it, evading its wheels and attacking its armor, although the most serious weapons they had were iron and wooden sticks.

I climbed up on the wall. Probably a minute after this one of the boys was shot. He was attacking (probably without any weapon) the vehicle from its rear; he came in contact with it, its door opened (probably from inside), and someone shot him to death at point blank range. He fell so that half of the body was inside the vehicle and the feet dragged on the ground. The vehicle continued moving back and forth, people were still attacking it, and those standing on the walls started screaming "Murderers!"

After a minute the boys picked up the body, which had fallen out. The vehicle was hitting the barricade, trying to make a hole in it; a trolley was crashed, but still it could not make a hole large enough to escape. Some reported later that it crushed two more people. I could not see this from where I stood, but there was a great danger and a real possibility for this.

Other vehicles stayed quiet, but there was general hysteria. A soldier from one of them ran out and raised his hands, appealing to the people and apologizing. From the walls people threw stones and sticks at the aggressive vehicles; then they took some gas from a car on the street and started throwing bottles of it. The vehicle began to burn on its top. It was shooting from the machine gun into the air. I could do nothing more with my placard and left the place when the vehicle began to burn.

Finally, two vehicles went back into the tunnel, where the people could not attack them from the walls above. Soldiers from three other vehicles surrendered with them and left their vehicles in the hands of the boys. Probably there were no more victims. When I visited that place an hour later, several members of parliament and a general who organized the defense of the building were there and they were negotiating with the soldiers. The situation had cooled down a bit, and even the excited teenagers were helping to introduce some order.

The Present Situation

But we were still expecting the general attack on the building, first at 2:00 A.M., then at 4:00 A.M., and I moved back closer to the major defense lines. The night came to an end quietly, although several times there were announcements about approaching troops. At 6:00 A.M. I returned home.

The present situation is unclear. The military made some more dangerous announcements on the official radio station. There are also rumors that the situation has improved greatly and that the plotters either escaped or were arrested. Anyway, there will be reason for me to go to the [parliament] building this evening. It is 4:00 A.M. now, the rain has stopped, and I am finishing this letter and going out.

P.S. I was informed that your letter to me of August 20 arrived. I have not read it yet. We—at least those who take an active interest in the event—have much information, including the leaflets, orders (both official and oppositional), free radio service (irregular), and free newspapers in the form of leaflets. The strangest thing is how easily and naturally people find themselves feeling and acting in the historical situation. As if it is ordinary life.

Azerbaijanis Remember the Day the Soviet Union Collapsed

Azerbaijan International

In the following viewpoint, eleven Azerbaijanis from all different walks of life and ranging in age from twenty to seventy-one describe their reactions when they first heard about the collapse of the Soviet Union. They go on to express their feelings about Azerbaijani freedom and the changes in their lives since their country became independent. Most say they were not shocked or surprised by the disintegration of the Soviet Union. Overall, most are pleased that their country is independent with its own flag and national anthem. Some are optimistic about the future. Others still feel nostalgia for the Soviet period and admit to having trouble getting used to the new system. Almost all are glad to be independent but confess that they are unhappy with

---

SOURCE. Matlab Alikishiyev, Vafa Mastanova, Khatira Hajiyeva, Sara Manafova, Arifa Mammadova, Amiraslan Aliyev, Zamana Gasimova, Vagif Nasirov, Aygun Valiyeva, Zulfugar Guliyev, and Abdulali Mammadov, "'Unthinkable': The Day the Soviet Union Collapsed," *Azerbaijan International*, Autumn 1999. © Azerbaijan International 1998. All rights reserved. Reproduced by permission.

the new lower standard of living, the low pay for most workers, and the way the city in which they live has changed.

On December 17, 1991, the leaders of four of the Soviet Republics—Ukraine, Belarus, Russia and Kazakhstan—met in the Belovezskaya Forest in Belarus and made an unprecedented announcement: the Soviet Union comprised of 15 Republics no longer existed as a unified entity.

For this issue, Farida Sadikhova asked Azerbaijanis how they had learned the news and what their initial thoughts and reactions had been. . . .

Matlab Alikishiyev, Crane Operator, 42

I wasn't shocked at all. I expected it after I witnessed the bloody events of January 1990 ["Black Saturday" or the "January Massacre" was an assault by the Soviet army on protesters, who were demonstrating to demand independence from the Soviet Union]. Everything happened right in front of my eyes. The Russians, who were like brothers to us during the Soviet period, sent their troops against us.

I worked as a crane operator in construction at that time. Beginning in early 1991, the projects became fewer and fewer—now there are none.

> When the Soviet Union collapsed, I thought: 'Maybe it's better to be free and independent.'

In the past, we used to build houses and give them to people for free. I worked as a crane operator for six years, and I was given an apartment for free. I thought that my children would work as I did and get an apartment for themselves. So I didn't worry about their future.

When the Soviet Union collapsed, I thought: "Maybe it's better to be free and independent. Maybe our work will move along faster." Now all that's left are my dreams.

Everything is so expensive these days. It's difficult to find work. During the Soviet period, I went to work in the morning and came back home in the evening, without ever worrying about my children's future. I was earning money and supporting my family. Now I get up in the morning wondering: What can I do today to earn some money to buy bread for my children?

> I never lose hope. Problems are temporary. I believe in a better future for all people.

I don't want to say that independence brought nothing to Azerbaijan. We have our national flag, our national anthem. We are establishing relations with other countries. All of this makes me happy, of course. But the standard of living for ordinary workers is very low. Anyway, I never lose hope. Problems are temporary. I believe in a better future for all people. . . .

Vafa Mastanova, Student, 20

I was 11 years old when the Soviet Union collapsed. I remember how our teachers used to tell us how strong we were and how other countries feared us. But when the news came, it didn't shock me or my family. For several years, demonstrators had been shouting "A-zad-lig," "A-zad-lig" ("Freedom," "Freedom") or its equivalent in many regions of the Soviet Union. So we weren't surprised; in fact, everybody in my family was glad. My father said, "Good. Now Azerbaijan can follow its own path and not have to depend on Russia or anybody else."

From that very first day of freedom up to the present day, I've felt many changes that are going on in my country. One of the first things that happened at school was that we started learning the new Latin alphabet. I was in the sixth grade. It felt strange to be learning the sounds and shapes of a new alphabet—just like first graders! We felt like babies! Soon afterwards, new textbooks appeared and the tri-colored flag and our national anthem were

> *Our people have suffered so much throughout the ages. Other countries have always had their hands on Azerbaijan.*

among the first pages. We started singing Azerbaijan's national anthem and raising the Azerbaijani flag.

I can't find words to express how it felt to see all those things happen. Our people have suffered so much throughout the ages. Other countries have always had their hands on Azerbaijan. It feels really great to be part of such an important moment in our history.

Khatira Hajiyeva, Historian, 33

The collapse of the Soviet Union was inevitable from a historical point of view. Like all other empires, the Soviet Empire was doomed to collapse. But still, when I heard a TV reporter announcing it, I was a bit shocked. I wondered: What's going to happen next? Which way will we take? Which ideas will shape our government?

Everything was so confusing. But later, when we had a chance to raise our own flag, to sing our national anthem, to value our mother tongue—I became so happy. I don't have nostalgia for the Soviet period. To be free and independent forever—that's what I wish for Azerbaijan.

Independence has given us many more choices. For example, when I was studying at the University, we were burdened with books by [Vladimir] Lenin and [Karl] Marx. We had to know them by heart, no matter how bored we were. We were clouded by Communist ideas. But now the youth have more choices. They can put forward their own ideas, not blindly serve others.

Sara Manafova, Artist, 67

I learned about the collapse of the Soviet Union while watching a session of the Milli Majlis (Parliament) on TV. I couldn't understand what the Parliament members were arguing about. Was it some kind of joke or something? How could such a great power come to an end? I couldn't believe it.

I had lived in the Soviet period my whole life and I liked my way of life. We 15 republics were like one big family. Now that family is divided, and each member lives separately; it's like a divorce.

I think the collapse was painful for most people—almost everyone I know seemed to be just as shocked as I was. We used to consider Moscow the capital of our Motherland. When we go there, we don't want to feel like strangers.

I'm still nostalgic for the old days. I was born and brought up during the Soviet period, and consider myself fortunate because of that. I can't get used to the new system. I think we've lost more than we've gained. . . .

Arifa Mammadova, University Professor, 50

When I first heard the news on TV, I was really shocked. I would never have thought that such a great power as the Soviet Union could ever cease to exist. At the same time, I felt relieved. It was like an innocent man finally escaping from prison. In the past, we were never allowed to make a single move by ourselves—always there were directives. So after the Union collapsed, we had hope for some radical changes in our lives. When the announcement came, I was very happy.

My first thought was: at last we'll be independent. But now as time has passed, I feel a kind of nostalgia, a yearning for the past. Such feelings are common here in Baku [capital of Azerbaijan].

During the Soviet period, our city was indescribably wonderful. But now it seems to me that the face of the city has changed. It's dirty. Street vendors are everywhere. Despite such difficulties, given the choice between living in the Soviet Union or in an independent Azerbaijan, without a doubt I would choose independence.

Amiraslan Aliyev, Head of a Scientific Lab, 50

Like many other people, I first heard the news on TV. I didn't expect it and thought it was something temporary. But that wasn't the case. The first thing I thought was: What kind of government will we establish? How will our lives change? How will I manage personally?

During the Soviet period, those who worked at the Academy of Sciences made decent salaries and didn't have to worry about money. But now our salaries are a mere pittance, and we're afraid of losing our jobs just like so many other people. Despite these difficulties that we're facing, I'm convinced that we'll eventually succeed. We, the older generation, built the Soviet Union; the youth must do their best now to build a strong, independent country.

Zamana Gasimova, Teacher, 47

I was shocked. For me the collapse of the Soviet Union was like a natural disaster—like a catastrophic storm at sea. My first thought was: What will we do if we're left alone? Will we be able to live independently?

Today Azerbaijan is an independent country with valuable resources: oil, gas and fertile soil. We can flourish if we use these things properly. But still I'm not completely satisfied with the conditions that we have today. I work at a school and my salary is too small.

I still feel very attached to the Soviet period as that's the way I was brought up. I would like to go back to it. But that doesn't mean that being independent is not good. On the contrary—I like it, but I would have to admit that I liked the Soviet period more. . . .

Vagif Nasirov, Athlete and Coach, 49

The collapse of the Soviet Union didn't happen in 1991. It began much earlier—in 1988, when relations between the nations in the Soviet Union began to deteriorate.

My parents were driven from their homes in Armenia that year, and the Union just closed its eyes to it. Then Armenia started an unjust war against Azerbaijan, claiming our territories. Again, the Union closed its eyes. Then Black January (1990) occurred. I knew that all of these unjust events would eventually lead to the collapse of the Soviet Union.

So when I heard the news on TV, I wasn't shocked at all. Of course, it was difficult to believe that such a great country could lose all of its power. As an athlete, the first thing I thought was: at last our sports will be independent. During the Soviet period, we used to join athletes from other republics to represent the Soviet Union. Whenever we won, the Soviet flag was hoisted, not our own Republic's flag. If you only knew how much I longed for that flag to be Azerbaijan's! Now I'm proud that our athletes can represent our own independent country.

Aygun Valiyeva, Teacher, 25

I was a 16-year-old schoolgirl when the Soviet Union collapsed. Everybody was talking about it—every house, every institution, every school. When we heard the news, we were shocked, especially my parents. They simply couldn't believe it.

The next day at school our first class was History. We discussed the events that were unfolding right in front of our eyes! Although our parents accepted the news as tragic, for us—the youth—it was fortunate and exciting.

Now we are independent. . . . When my parents talk about their nostalgia for the Soviet Union, I don't argue or criticize them—I know they spent the happiest moments of their lives during that time. But as for me, I prefer an independent Azerbaijan.

Still, there were a few things I liked better about the Soviet Union. I liked when we became Pioneers, then Komsomols [members of the Communist Union of Youth]. This program united all Soviet children. Unfortunately, nothing like that has yet replaced it today. But who knows, maybe in the future?

Zulfugar Guliyev, Welder, 37

We all talk about the "collapse" of the Soviet Union, but really it was more like a slow disintegration. In 1988 and 1989, when the national movement started in Azerbaijan, I joined it as well. Such movements were happening in other republics as well. That was one of the main reasons for the Soviet collapse.

> Even those who had higher positions were treated the same as the workers.

Another reason was that Russia supported Armenia when the Karabakh conflict broke out. When the Azerbaijani population of Karabakh was driven out of their homes and Moscow did not take any steps to prevent it, I knew that the Soviet Union could no longer exist and that it was already going downhill.

When I heard [Boris] Yeltsin's speech on TV announcing the dissolution of the Union, the first thing I thought was: What can we expect? What does it mean to be independent? We had grown so used to that system. We were afraid of the unknown—of living in another system that was completely unfamiliar to us.

I finished industrial trade school and worked as a welder. At that time there were four construction enterprises in Baku. I worked at the largest one. It's closed now and my heart aches.

Despite the fact that I didn't finish school, I was still given a three-room apartment and treated with respect. Even those who had higher positions were treated the same as the workers. Now I feel like nobody needs me.

Of course, it's good to be independent, to have our own flag, our own national anthem. But it's not good that thousands of workers go to so-called "slave markets" where they hope to be hired by the rich as very cheap labor. During the Soviet period, we didn't have such "markets." . . .

Abdulali Mammadov, Retiree, 71

I always feel nostalgic for the Soviet period. The Soviet power was built to help the poor and the helpless. It was the hope of the workers and peasants. There was equality everywhere and in everything. The rich do not share their wealth with the poor easily—that's why such a governing system was necessary. . . .

I'm not a politician to analyze the situation. I only compare my living conditions today with what I had back then. Let's consider the difference.

Education on all levels used to be free. Medical care was free. With my normal salary, I was able to take a vacation outside of Azerbaijan [to another part of the Soviet Union] at least once a year. I could buy a car and a summer home [dacha]. All the things I own today and all the things I ever achieved, took place during Soviet times.

But what can I do today on the pittance of my pension? The ideology of those years was that everybody should be compensated according to his capability. What's wrong with that? Today, we have to pay for everything—universities, medical services. What can people do with a measly $20–30 a month from their government salary?

A Teenage University Student Talks About Life in the New Russia

Ilya, as quoted in Deborah Adelman

In the following viewpoint, a Russian university student named Ilya describes his life in the new Russia—the work he does to make ends meet and the education he is receiving at the university. He shares his observations of the state of education in general and the attitudes and actions of the current generation of schoolchildren. He tells why he does not like some of the things going on in Russia at the moment, such as depolitization and the process of commercialization. He is especially unhappy about the effect they are having on science and culture. He views the breakup of the Soviet Union as natural and explains why he supports the government and why he believes people must be patient and better things will come. At the time of this interview, Ilya was nineteen years old and a fourth-year student of Russian language and literature at Moscow State University.

SOURCE. Deborah Adelman, "I Don't Like Living My Life According to the Plan/Ilya," *The "Children of Perestroika" Come of Age: Young People of Moscow Talk About Their Life in the New Russia*. 1994. Used by permission of M.E. Sharpe, Inc. Not for reproduction.

I have two more years at the university. I'm studying Russian literature, nineteenth-century. I went into the university with the idea that I wanted to get an education. I didn't know what I would do with it afterward. Of course, I would like to go on to work in the field I'm studying now at the university, but I am not at all certain that will be possible. It used to be that if a person got into the university, it was just assumed he'd go on and on, keep going in the same direction. But not now. . . .

Every now and then I get little part-time jobs, like translating American films. I did two films. I liked that work a lot. I'd be glad to do more. And in any case we're not going hungry. [My wife, Sasha, and I] get small student stipends, my father helps out every now and then, I get little jobs from time to time. We're managing. . . .

The State of Education

I'm satisfied at Moscow State University. A lot depends on me, of course, but I think the classes and the professors are good. I have a very good mentor, a senior professor who has been teaching for a long time, an interesting person, a teacher with a capital "T." He really gives me a lot. . . .

> The entire old order is being destroyed, something new is being built but it doesn't exist yet, and all of this has psychological consequences.

Unfortunately, I think the level at Moscow State is declining somewhat. The general breakdown here has reached such a profound level. It's the kind of time we're living through, a time of chaos and uncertainty. The entire old order is being destroyed, something new is being built but it doesn't exist yet, and all of this has psychological consequences. These changes aren't always good for culture as a whole, but in general I would say that the university is holding its own.

Schools in general aren't *sinking* to a very low level, they were *always* that way! But there are some very good schools developing now, with very original curricula. Of course you can count the number of those on your fingers. And when teachers start going on strike for higher pay, well . . . the schoolchildren are changing too. You can hear them. One says, "I'm Rambo." Another one says, "I'm the Terminator," "I'm a robot!" I can even see that the sixteen-year-olds in my old school are different from the way we were. Sometimes I visit my old school. Not long ago I was talking to some of my old teachers, and they were telling me that my graduating class was really the last one of the old type. . . .

Commercialization and Commerce on the Rise

My father and I had a little argument. He said he was afraid that there would be some kind of social explosion here, and I said to him, "No, nothing like that is going to happen here." But the worst battle that could take place here might be a women's revolution! My father thinks things here are a lot worse than I think they are. People here are tolerant, they can handle it. But of course it's possible that women won't take it anymore!

> I do support this government completely, because first of all I don't see that there is any alternative, anything better than what we have now.

We're going through the process of commercialization here, and even though I don't really like it, I know it's unavoidable. Things like having more money weren't that important in the past, but now, without more money you simply can't survive. There's also a general atmosphere of commerce that exists every place. You can see it on the street—people are selling things, reselling things. I have an acquaintance who finished the university, a very capable young man—he specialized in [the Nobel Prize–winning poet and writer Boris] Pasternak—and they were waiting for him to go work in the Pasternak Museum. But he didn't continue studying Pasternak; instead got involved in business, and not the highest sort of business, either!

The State of Things

What's going on now is very bad for science and culture. People are going into business, or leaving the country altogether, sometimes permanently, sometimes temporarily, to work. It's really a shame. We had some very high achievements in science and culture here, in spite of our horrible political system, but all of that is being lost now. There were good things here, too, and now, in spite of all the freedom, we're losing so many things. But I don't think it will go on this way much longer. Unless, God forbid, people's patience just runs out and things don't happen like they did last August.[*] Things won't go on like this. Personally, I feel skeptical about the current reforms. I don't think they're taking us in any specific direction. A lot of declarations are being made that I think are correct, and sometimes they even *do* some correct things, but there are a lot more declarations than anything else. . . .

Still, I do support this government completely, because first of all I don't see that there is any alternative, anything better than what we have now. And also, this might in fact be the type of government that with time could actually end up doing something, come up with some real reforms. But for now, well, look, prices have gone up, prices have been freed, and that's good; but it has to be connected with some real reforms in production, and so far that hasn't happened. Of course, they say they're doing that, but up to now they haven't. Probably they need time. It's normal for production to fall in the first stage of reform. . . .

The government is responsible for a great part of the problems. For example, taxes. They've raised taxes so high that production just isn't developing. It simply isn't profitable to open up a business. The goals are right, but

Poverty, homeless-
ness, and hunger
grew common in the
post-Soviet era. (Sergei
Guneyev/Time Life
Pictures/Getty Images.)

they have to take some very specific measures. The most important thing, of course, is privatization. Right now they privatize a factory as a formality, but in reality the same monopolists control it, even though on paper it's been privatized.

The price rises in January were really a shock. But the terrible thing is that this "January" just keeps going. Things are going up and up. You can take it for a while, a month, three months. But now, according [to] calculations by the International Monetary Fund, inflation is at 1,000 percent! And things could get worse!

The Coup and the Breakup of the Union

During the coup in August [1991] we were at the dacha [country house]. The night before the coup we had been sitting up with some friends, and, by chance, we were talking about things. For some reason I was in bad spirits. All of my optimism had left me, and I was cursing, saying how terrible things were, how awful it all was. In the morning our friend had to leave early to get to work, and he woke us up. So I said, "Seryozha, really, why are you doing this? Why did you have to wake us up so early?" And he said, "Listen, do you remember what we were talking about last night? Well, they've gotten rid of [President Mikhail] Gorbachev!" And I said, "Stop joking, it's not April Fool's Day!" But then we turned on the television and saw that it was true. Of course my mood really got low at first, even though at the same time I had the feeling that none of it was very serious. During the first hours of the coup I thought, "This can't last for long."

> It's not that things are quieter, it's just that people are fed up with talking about these things.

So Sasha and I went into Moscow from the dacha and in the subway I saw leaflets with [Boris] Yeltsin's call to resist—they were stuck on the walls with wheat paste. Sasha and I and my father all went to this huge meeting in front of the White House [parliament building]. But people weren't really all that upset. In the bus I even heard some people saying, well, that's what they needed to do with that Gorbachev! . . .

About the Soviet Union breaking up, I suppose on the one hand it sounds bad—after all, Europe is uniting and here we are, splitting up. If you look at it in the abstract, from the outside, of course, it is too bad. But the situation we had here, that kind of reality, well I think that the breakup is natural. The hope that something would change had already passed.

I think the students at the university care less about these things than they did [three years ago]. Three years ago was the time of newspapers, magazines, rallies, and demonstrations. And now it's just the opposite. There's a real depolitization now. And it's not that things are quieter, it's just that people are fed up with talking about these things.

Many students have just gotten involved with commercial matters—buying, reselling, that kind of thing. We have a bulletin board in our wing at school that's just full of advertisements that say I'm selling this, I'm buying that, etc. . . .

A Need to Wait and See

It seems to me that the best thing a person who supports this government can do at the moment is simply to endure a while longer. That is, the most progressive position to take at this point is to not be against this government, rather to just wait it out, have faith that something better will come. . . . The reforms are really not popular at the moment. It's not even so much that people are against the reforms as they are simply against the high prices! The material situation isn't even at the level it was at the beginning of perestroika. All the effort it takes to feed yourself, well, everybody has really grown tired. It's true that people are eating less than before. I can say that from my own experience. Little by little you get used to less. Somewhere along the way the standard became a different one. But all these things will pass.

As far as freedom is concerned, at least I can say that I am not limited in any way by anything. And as far as political parties, please! There are about eight hundred of them now in Russia. And some are important. I think our political life is going well enough. There are lots of newspapers, things like that. But of course there are economic problems, and full political freedom has an effect on the economic situation. Now there's been a wave of strikes—miners, doctors, teachers, and so on. . . .

Three years ago I was very full of hope. I think I didn't understand the difference between glasnost—freedom of speech—and freedom in general. Freedom in general happened after the coup, without a doubt. Up to that moment things were still very much under the control of the Communist Party, which was preventing the reforms from being carried out. I started saying that things were fine here too early, before they really were. But I'm not a pessimist now.

Note

* Ilya is referring to the August 1991 coup, and people's determination to defeat it by taking to the streets and erecting barricades.

CIS-Generation Teens Speak Out About the Soviet Union

Radio Free Europe/Radio Liberty

In the following viewpoint, four teenagers living in Kyrgyzstan, Tatarstan, Armenia, and Belarus, each born in December 1991, the month the Soviet Union collapsed and the Commonwealth of Independent States was formed, describe the impressions they have of life in the Soviet Union. Born when they were, they have no personal memories of what life was like in the Soviet Union; all of their views are based on reminiscences and stories passed on to them by their parents and grandparents. Among the positive notions they express are that getting a higher education was easier in the Soviet Union, a person did not have to work as hard to succeed, living conditions and prices were better, and young people their age had more privileges.

SOURCE. "CIS: The Generation That Never Knew the Soviet Union," *Radio Free Europe/Radio Liberty*, December 8, 2006. Reprinted with the permission of Radio Free Europe/Radio Liberty, 1201 Connecticut Ave., N.W., Washington DC 20036, www.rferl.org.

On December 8, 1991, the leaders of Russia, Belarus, and Ukraine gathered at a site in the Belarusian forest of Belavezhskaya Pushcha to declare that the Soviet Union was dead.

In its place, they announced the formation of a new alliance, the Commonwealth of Independent States. For those who lived through it, it was a heady but uncertain time. Hopes of social change and political freedom mixed with fears of economic freefall and the disintegration of state institutions. But what about those with no memory of that time?

> 'I had heard that the Soviet Union was dissolved in December 1991. My parents tell me about that time a lot.'

RFE/RL [Radio Free Europe/Radio Liberty] spoke to young people born in December 1991 and living in the former USSR about their experiences as the first post-Soviet generation.

Jangyl and Ayrat

"I had heard that the Soviet Union was dissolved in December 1991. My parents tell me about that time a lot," says Jangyl Tashbayeva, who was born on December 27 in the city of Osh, in southern Kyrgyzstan. "There was a lot of hardship at that time. Instead of helping each other, people at that time thought only about their own fate. It was a very hard time."

"I know about communism through what I heard from my parents and grandparents," says 15-year-old Ayrat, who grew up in Tatarstan. "I heard that in the [general secretary of the Communist Party from 1964 to 1982, Leonid] Brezhnev era, life was easier because it was a calm time. But if you consider the period before Brezhnev, for example the [general secretary of the Communist Party from 1922 to 1953, Joseph] Stalin and [the first head of the Soviet Union Vladimir] Lenin eras, it was harder for people due to mass repression. So I'd choose the Brezhnev era to live in, because that was the calmest time."

Born thousands of miles apart, the only thing these teenagers share is the month of their birth—December 1991.

Inga

It was the month the Soviet Union collapsed, the Commonwealth of Independent States was formed, and life as many people knew it was changed forever.

Inga Ghukasyan was born December 4 in the Armenian capital Yerevan, where she still lives with her parents—her engineer father, Edik, and her mother, Marina, a mathematician.

A pretty 15-year-old with long dark hair, Ghukasyan is growing up in a different world than her parents.

She studies English instead of Russian, is already intent upon becoming an economist, and looks to herself—rather than the state—to ensure her success in a highly competitive educational environment.

"I have heard from my parents that getting a higher education was easier and living conditions were better then than they are now. I think when my parents were my age, they had more privileges than I do. Living now is a struggle; you have to work hard to succeed," Inga says. "In their school years, my parents had no problem entering a university and gaining a profession with the base knowledge they acquired in school. But for me, though now I study hard at school, I can't enter university unless I have private classes to get prepared for my entrance exams."

Jangyl

Other CIS teenagers have inherited similarly positive notions of life in the Soviet Union.

Jangyl's father was a tradesman in Soviet times, but now owns a store in Bishkek. Her mother, likewise, gave up her Soviet-era career as a nurse to work as a shop assistant.

Jangyl, the second of three children who says her favorite hobbies are music and dancing, says her parents sometimes speak fondly of the Soviet Union. . . .

"They say good things. For instance, before 1991 they were able to buy a lot of things for one *som* [Soviet ruble]. It was much better than the prices we have today. A box of matches was just a *tyiyn* [Soviet kopek]. For one *som*, they used to be able to fill an entire basket. They could buy all their food for one *som*," Jangyl says.

Aleh

For Aleh Sushko, a 15-year-old living in Belarus, it wasn't money that was a problem for his parents. It was finding something to buy with it.

"They've told me that the situation in 1991 was very difficult. In order to buy food, they needed to stand in very long lines. At that time [people] had money, but there was nothing to buy. And now it's the other way. You can buy almost everything but you don't have the money to do it," Aleh says.

Aleh's birthday is December 8, the day the Soviet Union was formally declared defunct. He lives with his parents in a modest two-room apartment in Zialony Luh, a suburb of Minsk. The family does not have a car or a dacha [country home], but they do have several bicycles, a piano, and shelves filled with rows and rows of books.

Parents Speak: The Good and the Bad

For children born in December 1991, the 15 years of post-Soviet life are all they've ever known. But what was it like for the parents who saw their children come into the world just as the USSR was falling apart?

> 'We didn't stop to think about the impact [becoming independent] would have on our children's lives.'

In Yerevan, Inga's father, Edik Ghukasyan, said it was a difficult time to bring a child into the world.

"I remember December 1991. Awful times. . . . We had no electricity, it was very cold, and we had very bad living conditions. The Soviet Union had collapsed and Armenia had become a newly independent state," Edik says. "Everyone in Armenia was going out to join street protests. We wanted to be independent, and then we were, and we were very glad for that. . . . We didn't stop to think about the impact it would have on our children's lives. It was something that needed to happen, and it happened."

Belarus under autocratic leader Alyaksandr Lukashenka has, more than other former republics, maintained a Soviet-style characteristic. But it has seen dramatic changes as well.

Aleh's mother, 41-year-old Iryna, says the years following the collapse of the Soviet Union have been a mix of good and bad: "Everyday life has perhaps become better when we compare it to the perestroika [restructuring] years. At that time it was so difficult to get food and clothes for babies; you could only get them with coupons. But morally, it was better at the beginning. [Now] the Soviet [state] symbols have returned, Stalin has once again become a hero in Belarus, [and] history and the constitution are being rewritten."

In Kyrgyzstan, Jangyl Tashbayeva's parents say that despite the difficulties of the time, they're happy to have brought a child into a rapidly changing world.

Jangyl's mother, Maria, says she and her husband saw an independent Kyrgyzstan as a chance to give their daughter a secure future.

"Now every person has started to fight for his own life. If Kyrgyzstan can stand on its own feet, we hope it will be good for the lives of our children. Now we have both the good life and hardship, coexisting at the same time."

GLOSSARY

Afgantsy Veterans of the Soviet-Afghanistan war.

apparatchiks Russian colloquial term for persons occupied full time in the work of the Communist Party of the Soviet Union (CPSU) and/ or the republic communist parties.

Baltic States The countries of Estonia, Latvia, and Lithuania.

Bolsheviks Revolutionaries who, under the leadership of Vladimir Lenin, formed the Russian Communist Party in 1918 and began calling themselves Communists.

capitalism Economic system characterized by private ownership of business.

Cold War Attempt after World War II by the Soviet Union and the United States to gain world influence by means short of full-scale war.

Commonwealth of Independent States Confederation of former Soviet republics established in 1991 by Russia, Ukraine, and Belarus to oversee common interests in the economies, foreign policy, and defense of its members.

communism Social system characterized by common ownership of the means of production and the absence of social class; official ideology of the Soviet Union.

Communist Party of the Soviet Union (CPSU) Official name of the Communist Party in the Soviet Union, which until 1991 ruled every aspect of Soviet life.

Congress of People's Deputies Highest legislative and executive authority in the Soviet Union.

Congress of Soviets Ruling body of the Soviet state until 1963; revived in 1989.

Coup of 1991	Failed attempt in August 1991 by hard-line Soviet Communist leaders to bring down Soviet President Mikhail Gorbachev and his reforms.
czar	Name for the ruler of Russia until 1917.
dacha	Russian country house used most often in the summer.
Duma	Russian parliament.
glasnost	Soviet government cultural and social policy of the late 1980s that encouraged open discussion of political and social issues and freer distribution of news and information.
Kremlin	Seat of the government of Russia and formerly the Soviet government.
KGB	Committee for State Security, the Soviet state security police organization established in 1954.
Mensheviks	A moderate Marxist group within the Russian revolutionary movement who believed that socialism should be achieved gradually using parliamentary methods.
nomenklatura	Bureaucratic elites in political favor, such as Communist Party officials (above all, Party secretaries), government officials, and senior officers in the Soviet armed forces.
perestroika	Soviet government reform policy of the late 1980s to economically and socially restructure the Soviet Union.
Politburo	Principal policy-making body of the Soviet Union.
proletariat	Working class.
putsch	Coup, or sudden planned attempt to overthrow a government using military force.
Soviet	Committee or council formed by Russian revolutionaries to represent the people.

State Emergency Committee	Group of eight high-level Soviets, including the USSR vice president, prime minister, head of the KGB, minister of defense, head of the Association of State Enterprises, minister of the interior, chair of the Soviet farmers' union, and head of the military-industrial complex and deputy chair of the Defense Council, who initiated the Coup of 1991.
Supreme Soviet	Overall council governing the entire Soviet Union from 1963 to 1991.
Treaty of Brest-Litovsk	Separate World War I peace treaty signed in 1918 by Soviet Russia and the Central Powers that ended Russian involvement in the war.
Union of Soviet Socialist Republics (USSR)	Soviet state made up of fifteen constituent or union republics in Eastern Europe and northern Asia; also known as the Soviet Union.
White House	Government building in Moscow.

CHRONOLOGY

1917	Bolsheviks overthrow the government. Tsar Nicholas II abdicates, and Vladimir Lenin becomes the head of the Central Committee.
1918	The Treaty of Brest-Litovsk is signed.
1922	The Union of Soviet Socialist Republics (USSR) is established; Joseph Stalin becomes the general secretary of the Communist Party of the Soviet Union.
1933	Diplomatic relations are established with the United States.
1936	Kazakhstan and Kirgizia become Soviet republics.
1939	The western portions of Ukraine and Belarus are incorporated into the Soviet Union.
1940	The Soviet Union annexes Estonia, Latvia, and Lithuania.
1941	Germany invades the Soviet Union, setting off the Great Patriotic War (Russian name for World War II).
1945	World War II ends; the Soviet Army occupies much of Eastern Europe and the eastern part of Germany; the Soviet Union emerges from the war as a superpower.
1952	The All-Union Communist Party (Bolsheviks) becomes the Communist Party of the Soviet Union (CPSU).

1953   Joseph Stalin dies; Nikita Khrushchev becomes the first secretary of the Communist Party of the Soviet Union.

1964   Nikita Khrushchev is removed from power; Leonid Brezhnev becomes first secretary of the Communist Party of the Soviet Union.

1966   Leonid Brezhnev's title changes from first secretary to general secretary.

1979   Soviet troops invade Afghanistan.

1982   Leonid Brezhnev dies and is replaced by KGB (Committee for State Security) chief Yuri Andropov.

1984   Yuri Andropov dies and is replaced by Konstantin Chernenko.

1985   Mikhail Gorbachev becomes general secretary after the death of Konstantin Chernenko and begins an anti-alcohol campaign.

1987   Mikhail Gorbachev proposes perestroika, a program of economic, political, and social restructuring, and glasnost, a policy of openness.

1988   Mikhail Gorbachev challenges nationalists in Kazakhstan, the Baltic republics, Armenia, and Azerbaijan.

1989   The last of the Soviet troops withdraw from Afghanistan; nationalist riots are put down in Georgia; the Communist Party of Lithuania declares its independence from the Soviet Communist Party; the Cold War ends; the Congress of People's Deputies is created.

1990   The Congress of People's Deputies votes to end the

Communist Party's control over the government and elects Mikhail Gorbachev as president of the Soviet Union; the Baltic states of Estonia, Latvia, and Lithuania announce their independence; Boris Yeltsin is elected president of the Russian Soviet Federative Socialist Republic and resigns from the CPSU; Ukraine, Armenia, Turkmenistan, and Tajikistan declare independence; free local elections are held in the USSR.

April 1991 Mikhail Gorbachev draws up a new treaty for the republics of the Soviet Union.

August 1991 High-ranking Soviet officials form the State Committee for the State of Emergency, detain president Gorbachev at his holiday villa, and initiate an unsuccessful coup attempt against Gorbachev; Boris Yeltsin bans the CPSU on Russian soil and seizes its assets; Mikhail Gorbachev resigns as CPSU general secretary and dissolves the CPSU; the Ukraine and then other republics declare independence.

September 1991 The Congress of People's Deputies votes to dissolve the Soviet Union.

December 1991 The leaders of Russia, the Ukraine, and Belarus sign the Minsk Agreement, ending the USSR and replacing it with the Commonwealth of Independent States (CIS); the Russian government takes over offices of the USSR in Russia; Mikhail Gorbachev resigns as Soviet president and announces the end of the USSR; the United States recognizes the independence of the remaining Soviet republics.

FOR FURTHER READING

Books

Stephen F. Cohen and Katrina Vanden Heuvel, *Voices of Glasnost: Conversations with Gorbachev's Reformers*. New York: Norton, 1989.

Fred Coleman, *The Decline and Fall of the Soviet Empire: Forty Years That Shook the World, from Stalin to Yeltsin*. New York: St. Martin's Press, 1996.

Robert Daniels, *The End of the Communist Revolution*. New York: Routledge, 1993.

Daniel C. Diller, *Russia and the Independent States*. Washington, DC: Congressional Quarterly, 1993.

Gregory Feifer, *Great Gamble: The Soviet War in Afghanistan*. New York: HarperCollins, 2009.

Neil Felshman, *Gorbachev, Yeltsin, and the Last Days of the Soviet Empire*: New York: St. Martin's Press, 1992.

Marc Garcelon, *Revolutionary Passage: From Soviet to Post-Soviet Russia, 1985–2000*. Philadelphia: Temple University Press, 2005.

Mikhail Gorbachev, *The August Coup: The Truth and the Lessons*. New York: HarperCollins, 1991.

Andrei S. Grachev, *Final Days: The Inside Story of the Collapse of the Soviet Union*. Boulder, CO: Westview, 1995.

Ryszard Kapuscinski, *Imperium*. New York: Knopf Doubleday, 1995.

Andrew Langley, *The Collapse of the Soviet Union: The End of an Empire*. Minneapolis, MN: Compass Point Books, 2007.

Melvyn P. Leffler, *For the Soul of Mankind: The United States, the Soviet Union, and the Cold War*. New York: Farrar, Straus and Giroux, 2008.

David Marples, *The Collapse of the Soviet Union, 1985–1991*. Harlow, UK: Longman, 2004.

Jack F. Matlock, Jr., *Autopsy on an Empire: The American Ambassador's Account of the Collapse of the Soviet Union*. New York: Random House, 1995.

George J. Neimanis, *The Collapse of the Soviet Empire: A View from Riga*. Westport, CT: Praeger, 1997.

David Remnick, *Lenin's Tomb: The Last Days of the Soviet Empire*. New York: Random House, 1993.

Robert Service, *Russia: Experiment with a People*. Cambridge, MA: Harvard University Press, 2003.

Hedrick Smith, *The New Russians*. New York: Random House, 1990.

William E. Watson, *The Collapse of Communism in the Soviet Union*. Westport, CT: Greenwood Press, 1998.

Boris Nikolayevich Yeltsin, *Midnight Diaries*. New York: Public Affairs, 2000.

Periodicals

David Aikman, "What If the Soviet Union Collapses?" *Time*, December 25, 1989.

"Back to the U.S.S.R.?" *Harper's Magazine*, July 1996.

Ellen Barry, "As Soviet Union Dissolved, Enclave's Fabric Unraveled," *New York Times*, September 7, 2008.

Michael Binyon, "The Chain Reaction That Toppled Communism," *Times*, June 4, 2009.

Stephen Castle, "European Union to Reach Out to 6 Former Soviet States in Meeting," *New York Times*, May 5, 2009.

George J. Church, James Carney, Ann M. Simmons, and Bruce van Voorst, "Postmortem Anatomy of a Coup," *Time*, September 2, 1991.

James F. Clarity, "End of the Soviet Union: On Moscow's Streets, Worry and Regret," *New York Times*, December 26, 1991.

Robert V. Daniels, "Was Communism Reformable?" *Nation*, January 3, 2000.

David R. Francis, "New Insights on the Soviet Union's Collapse," *Christian Science Monitor*, July 23, 2007.

Cal Fussman, "Mikhail Gorbachev," *Esquire*, September 2008.

Ken Gluck, "The New Russian Imperialists," *Nation*, September 14, 1992.

Paul Gregory, "How the Soviet System Cracked," *Policy Review*, October-November, 2008.

James G. Hershberg, "Just Who Did Smash Communism?" *Washington Post*, June 27, 2004.

Geoffrey Hosking, "Rulers and Victims: The Russians in the Soviet Union," *History Today*, April 2006.

Flora Lewis, "A Union Is Born, a Union Dies," *New York Times*, December 13, 1991.

Per Manson, "Back in the USSR," *History Today*, October 1, 1997.

Andrew Nagorski, "Kissing Up to the Past," *Newsweek*, June 10, 1996.

Bruce W. Nelan, Paul Hofheinz, John Kohan, and J.F.O. McAllister, "Once a Gray Monolith," *Time*, March 12, 1990.

John O'Sullivan, "Margaret Thatcher's Legacy of Freedom," *USA Today Magazine*, March 2009.

Serge Schmemann, "Declaring Death of Soviet Union, Russia and 2 Republics Form New Commonwealth," *New York Times*, December 9, 1991.

David K. Shipler, "After the Coup," *New Yorker*, November 11, 1991.

Michael Specter, "Russian Parliament Denounces Soviet Union's Breakup," *New York Times*, March 16, 1996.

E.M. Swift and Jeff Lilley, "Soviet Disunion," *Sports Illustrated*, July 13, 1992.

Tatyana Tolstaya, "Mikhail Gorbachev," *Time: The Time 100*, April 13, 1998.

Helen Womack, "Coming Full Circle 25 Years Later," *Moscow Times*, May 22, 2009.

Web Sites

Interstate Statistical Committee of the Commonwealth of Independent States (www.cisstat.com/eng). This Web site provides statistical and background information about the Commonwealth and its member states, as well as links to press releases and publications.

Seventeen Moments in Soviet History (www.soviethistory .org). This Web site contains an archive of texts, images, maps, and audio and video materials from the Soviet period from 1917 to 1991.

INDEX